A Catcher's Companion:

The World of Holden Caulfield

Second Edition: Revised and corrected

by Sean McDaniel

A Catcher's Companion

Lit. Happens Publishing,
Santa Monica, California 90405

If you purchase this book without a cover you should be aware that you are not getting your money's worth. The cover is pretty and helps keep the loose pages from flopping around and getting lost. While it is not clear why anyone would pull the cover off of a book and try to sell it that way, it is important that you know this book once had one and you didn't get it.

If you are reading this book on an e-reader you may ignore the above advice.

Lit. Happens Publishing Edition

Second Edition, 2019

This ***OP Publishing*** edition is published by arrangement with the author.

Distributed by men and women in trucks.

Printed in the United States of America and elsewhere.

10 9 8 7 6 5 4 3 2

For OLvia, Eva
And my mentor in all things worth doing,
my father, Roderick McDaniel.

A Catcher's Companion:
The World of Holden Caulfield

Introduction

The story is a familiar one and probably as old as courtship: Someone meets someone else and forms a romantic atttachment. At some point one invites the other to meet "the family" over dinner. At the appointed date and time all required participants are in their places; the food is good, the company is congenial, everyone smiles, tells amusing stories and passes the grits. But something is wrong: What are these people talking about? Who are Lena, "Gabby", "Little Bo" and this Uncle Marcus whose name occasions a rolling of the eyes? What alarming thing happened in Winslow, Arizona years earlier? Why does the repetition of the phrase "fit and trim" cause such general mirth and why is younger brother Phillip so pleased to be the only person at the table with a blue plate, and a chipped one at that? There seems to be only one person present who does not know the answers to these questions and that person is *you*, the invited guest.

It's nobody's fault. Every family has its own history and jargon, quite independent of the rest of the world. You just dropped in a few years (or decades) too late to have acquired all the necessary information. You're still welcome, fed, and included in the conversation, but, like a dim, distant uncle from out-of-town, always fall just a little bit short of full participation.

This analogy compares well to the experience of reading many great novels. You know you've been invited and are welcome, but can't help but feel you lack the necessary background to be a full participant. The feeling is no less real whether you are reading Mark Twain, Henry James or F. Scott Fitzgerald. Even a so-called "modern" novel can defy our most earnest attempts at assimilation. Take James Joyce's *Ulysses* (Please.) J.D. Salinger's *The Catcher in the Rye* is, for all its popularity, one of those novels.

Salinger's only novel, universally regarded as a modern classic, appears on the required reading lists of virtually every high school in the country. Each year a quarter of a million people read it for the first time, most of them between the ages of fifteen and twenty-five. What with the passage of time, virtually all of these readers lack a familiarity with the people, places, and terminology of the 1940's without which much of the novel's unique color is lost. Sixty years is a substantial passage of time. Figures of speech, music, films, customs, geography and public personalities of the late 1940's are now quite obscure to those born after 1980. (When I was in high school I considered WWII ancient history, yet at the time only 20 years separated me from the Battle of the Bulge.) Add to this the fact that increasing numbers of young Americans are coming to this novel from other cultures entirely. If scarcely one native-born student out of twenty can define "galoshes", it's hard to expect an English language learner from the Ukraine to automatically understand an expression like "chew the rag".[1] When many of the props Holden uses to tell his story or fix the time and place of his odyssey have been stripped of their meaning the reader

---

[1] *The Catcher in the Rye* has been published in more than 70 editions and 30 languages worldwide.

is left with an experience that pales against that of a culturally-assimilated, literate adult reader of the 1950's. *A Catcher's Companion: The World of Holden Caulfield* is intended to help fill-out the missing context and make the reader a regular member of the family.

There is no question that *The Catcher in The Rye* ranks as an important book; its fictional protagonist, Holden Caulfield is as much a shaper and reflection of late twentieth century adolescent awareness as any character from *"The Breakfast Club", "Rebel Without a Cause"* or *"Ferris Bueller's Day Off"*. A novel that never rose higher than fourth place on the best seller lists in 1951-52 and was not even one of the top ten best-selling novels in its year of publication has become, by almost any measure, one of the most influential novels of the twentieth century.

More recently *The Catcher in the Rye* has become as well known for it obsessive adherents as its literary worth. Holden Caulfield fanatics range all the way from otherwise normal folks who set up "Catcher" web sites, name their twins Phoebe and Allie or have CACHRYE put on their vanity license plates, to real psychos like that guy who had John Lennon autograph his copy before murdering him, the priveledged white boy who felt it was a necessary piece of equipment when he arrived in Los Angeles to stalk, and eventually murder, actress Rebecca Schaeffer, and the damaged loser who tried to impress actress Jodie Foster by assassinating President Ronald Reagan (and failed at both). But saying that a few social misfits were fond of *The Catcher in the Rye* is by no means a fair comment on the novel's content or literary worth. Delusional personalities, those afflicted with various psychoses, are ill equipped for literature; the author's ideas and intent are lost in the rage and howl of inner demons. *Winnie the Pooh* might as well be *Last Exit to Brooklyn*. It goes without saying that most of these extremists have either missed the point of the novel or read something into it that is not there, but the fact that a novel has been molded by readers as much as it has molded them is one of the remarkable qualities shared by those few novels which have also become social phenomena.

Reading *The Catcher in the Rye* in high school is for many students as much a rite of passage as detention and prom. For some it is all they'll remember ten years later. As early as 1961 "Catcher" was appearing widely on secondary school recommended reading lists. By 1981 it was the second most frequently taught novel in American secondary schools. In spite of regular challenges by school boards and special interest groups it remains in the top ten in both public and parochial schools across the country.

In the years that I taught literature I never tired of introducing students to what I still think is an artful, accessible and emotionally sincere work of fiction of surprising depth with passages of genuine humor that still retain the power to generate laughter. I never tired of rereading it, aloud or at home as I prepared for the next day's discussion. While certainly a reflection of a very particular time and place, there is in *The Catcher in the Rye* the universality that any enduring work of fiction must possess and, in spite of the first-person vernacular in which the story is told, a surprising depth to the prose. Of course, some students didn't care for the book or its protagonist. More than once I've heard him denounced as a lazy, over-privileged whiner[2], but most enjoyed their first experience with the novel. I was fine with that; it is after all just a really good novel, not tablets from Sinai.

I used to tell my students, "Times change, fashions change, language changes, but *people* don't". I still believe this, but I also know that those things that do change can make a full understanding of human behavior difficult. So, often I found myself drawn into mini-lessons on the significance of the Biltmore Clock, what the Radio City Music Hall is, the phrase "give her the time", or the identities of "the Lunts". Though I confess to secretly having enjoyed these digressions, there is no question that they usually brought the narrative or the discussion of literary technique to an abrupt halt. It was at these times that I began to see the need for this book.

---

[2] Hamlet has also been similarly disparaged.

The purpose of what follows is not to interpret or explain what J.D. Salinger has written, and by no means do I wish to delve more than cursorily into the author's biography or other fictional works. This book is designed primarily for readers who have no way of knowing as much about life in post-WW II America in New York as Salinger or readers who bought *The Catcher in the Rye* on its 1951[3] publication did. If you are looking for a commentary on the novel, critical responses, chapter-by-chapter synopses or interpretation there are plenty of other sources for that information. The fact is, I don't think this book really needs a lot of interpretation. There is nothing going on in this novel that a thoughtful reading will not reveal. If, however, you wish to enhance your understanding of *The Catcher in the Rye* with accessible notes on the "lost" culture of Holden's world I think you'll find what you need right here. After all, you've been invited to sit at the table with a very interesting young man.

Note: I am only a reader of *The Catcher in the Rye*. I have made no contribution to it, do not suggest that I possess any unique insight into its genesis, and can claim no relationship whatsoever with the author. What follow are my opinions, interpretations and the results of my reading in this novel and other works of fiction and nonfiction. With the exception of occasional, very brief excerpts from the text used to identify specific points I would like to clarify or explicate all of what follows is my own.

If, at times, I seem to be talking about Holden Caulfield as if he were a real person that is because I think it is the least a character who has endured the age of sixteen for more than fifty years deserves.

Another Note: These annotations are organized by their original chapter number in the sequence in which they occur in the text. Page numbers correspond to the *Bantam* and *Little, Brown and Company* paperback editions that are virtually identical.

---

[3] *The Catcher in the Rye* was first published in July of 1951. It cost $3.00.

And Still Another Note: There is no denying that this is a book written about a white boy by a white man at a time when very few readers bothered to consider the ramifications of that. Because I know of many instances where non-white, non-male readers have found the arc of Holden's journey relevant and interesting I would like to believe that there is a universality to his story that transcends gender, race and ethnicity. But I can't know for sure and feel confident that this aspect of the work will be, or has been, the subject of someone else's thoughtful dissertation. The reader will have to determine for himself/herself whether this novel "matters", today.

The Cover

Author, J.D. Salinger was never completely happy with the cover of the original edition. Designed by Michael Mitchell, the dust jacket of the first American edition featured a stylized carousel horse superimposed over an image of central park and the Manhattan skyline.

Though artful in a distinctly "mid-century" way Salinger disputed the need for pictorial representation of any sort. Equally offensive in the author's eyes was the cover art of the first British edition, a grey-green watercolor wash sentimentally depicting an energetic Phoebe rushing from Holden to the carousel.

Worst of all by Salinger's standard was the sentimental artwork on the front of the 1953 Signet paperback edition. The cover painting featuring a stolid-looking Holden in an overcoat and his signature red hunting hat passing before a seedy Times Square tableaux was by the now-revered James Avati who painted some of Bantam's "golden-age" covers in the 1940's and 50's. Though he was good enough for Drieser, Faulkner and Isherwood, his vision wasn't at all acceptable in Salinger's eyes. According to Avati, however, Salinger was

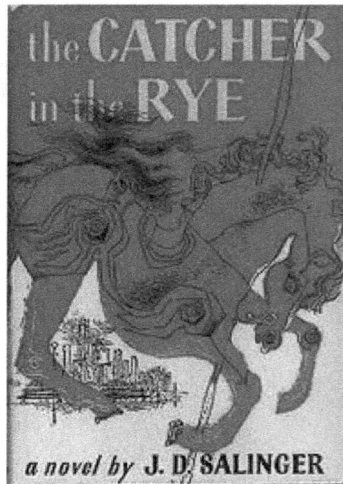

willing to go with a more sentimental approach if graphic depiction was seen as absolutely necessary.

It wasn't until the 1964 Bantam edition that Salinger got what he had wanted all along: a plain oxblood cover (a shade he had specifically requested) adorned with only the title and the author's name. With the exception of Little, Brown and Company's hardbound edition, which still carries the original

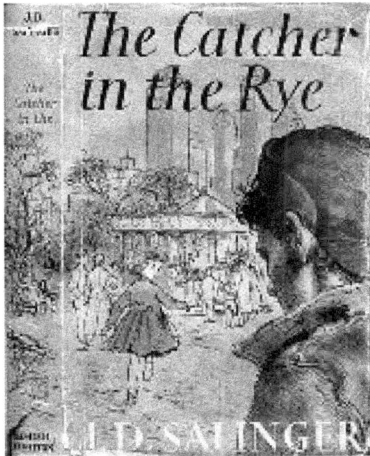

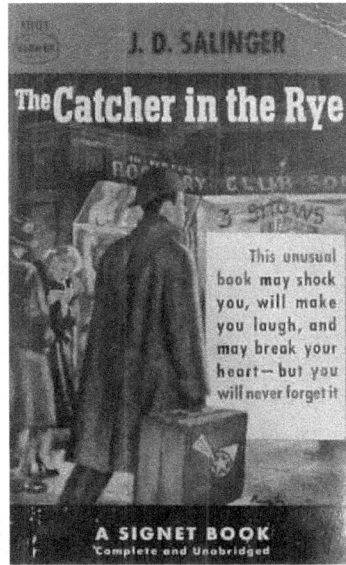

cover art, all subsequent editions have been equally austere.

Title page

The Catcher in the Rye

The title of this novel arises from Holden Caulfield's misunderstanding of a traditional song based on a poem by Robert Burns.

Robert Burns (1579-1596) is Scotland's most popular poet. He wrote hundreds of poems in his lifetime though only a few dozen are regularly anthologized today. You will hear his lyric to "Auld Lang Syne" every year on December 31st just before the stroke of midnight.

The title of John Steinbeck's novel *Of Mice and Men* comes from Burns' poem, "To a Mouse On Turning Up Her Nest with a Plow".[4]

The poem, "Comin' Thro The Rye[5]" was written in 1796 and shortly afterward applied to a melody in order to give inebriated Scots an excuse to whip out the old bagpipes. The ditty tells of a rather plain girl who is virtually ignored in town, but clearly very popular with the young men she encounters out in the fields. If you want to hear it, Google it.

On its face this poem has nothing whatsoever to do either with Holden, New York, or Central Park, though I suppose one might draw a tentative link between a drinking song and

---

[4] Though he is known to have written "To a Mouse, On Turning Up Her Nest with a Plow", and "To a Louse", he is unlikely to have received a reply in either case.

[5] Rye is a grass cultivated for its grain, like wheat. It can be ground into a flour, used as animal feed or mixed with water and fermented into beer or liquor.

Holden's constant quest for a cocktail. The lyric does not appear in the novel until Chapter 16, p. 115 and it is not discussed until Holden explains his ideal occupation to his sister Phoebe in Chapter 22, p. 173.

This song is in the public domain (see "**Chapter 1: David Copperfield**" below) so you may sing it to your hearts content without fear of being sued by Mr. Burns or his heirs.

Comin' Thro' The Rye

Gin a body meet a body
Comin' thro' the rye
Gin a body kiss a body
Need a body cry?
Ilka lassie has her laddie
Nane, they say, hae I
Yet a' the lads they smile at me
When comin' thro' the rye.
Gin a body meet a body
Comin' frae the town
Gin a body kiss a body
Need a body frown?
Ilka lassie has her laddie
Nane, they say, hae I
Yet a' the lads they smile at me
When comin' thro' the rye.
'Mang the train there is a swain
I dearly lo'e myself
But what his name or whaur his hame
I dinna care to tell
Ilka lassie has her laddie
Nane, they say, hae I
Yet a' the lads they smile at me
When comin' thro' the rye.

Holden has lived to the age of sixteen believing that the lyric goes, "If a body *catch* a body comin' though the rye". He is wrong, of course, and his precocious sister Phoebe corrects him (**Chapter 22; page 224**). Yet, based on this error, Holden has created a picture in his mind of "all these little kids playing...in this big field of rye". When children play too close to the edge they, like Disney's bogus lemmings[6], need a catcher to keep them from falling into the abyss. The catcher is, of course, Holden Caulfield.

An interesting parallel to Holden's ideosyncratic vision is Robert Browning's version of the ancient story of "*The Pied Piper of Hamelin* ". In this poem, which Holden certainly read in English class somewhere between "Lord Randall, My Son" and *The Return of the Native,* the Piper, who has successfully rid Hamelin town of rats as per his promise, is so angered by the Mayor's refusal to pay him the promised thousand guilders that

---

[6] The story of Disney's suicidal lemmings is one of the more interesting bits of widespread modern mythology. In the late 1950's Walt Disney Productions created several "documentaries" they grouped under the title of "True Life Adventures". These films were incorporated into the weekly anthology series, *Disneyland*, later re-named *Walt Disney's Wonderful World of Color.* One 1958 production was *White Wilderness,* ostensibly the story of a year in the frozen north. A dramatic segment showed hundreds of the furry lemmings hurling themselves off a cliff into the sea in an inexplicable act of instinct gone wild. The film's narrator, Winston Hibbler, tells us that a "kind of compulsion seizes each tiny rodent and, carried along by an unreasoning hysteria, each falls into step for a march that will take them to a strange destiny." The little creartures, now "victims of an obsession (act on) a one-track thought: Move on! Move on!" So "over they go, casting themselves out bodily into space." The end result, shown vividly while funereal Disney-music plays behind, is a sea littered with lemming corpses bobbing in the waves.
The problem was that none of this is based on fact. There is no certainty as to where the filmmakers got the idea for their lemming episode, but wildlife biologists agree that there is no truth to the mass suicide myth. The filmmakers reportedly imported lemmings to Alberta, Canada, where the filming was taking place and staged the whole thing. Millions of people saw it on television Sunday evening and the next thing you know it became truth. The film was subsequently re-edited for distribution through Disney's educational films division and for the next two decades thousands of school children who may have missed the original broadcast were reacquainted with the compelling, but utterly fictitious, insight into the mysteries of nature. To this day the phrase "march like lemmings" is used as a metaphor for inexplicably self-destructive mass behavior.

he steals all of the town's children. He pipes a tune so seductive and enticing that every child within hearing range follows him in a jolly morris-dance out of town, past the river Weser and through a cleft in the side of Koppleburg Hill. When all - except one, poor lame boy - have entered, the crevice closes up behind them. (Apparently Hamelin was seriously out of compliance with handicapped access ordinances.) The lonely child returns to his home to report the Piper's alluring promise of

> ...a joyous land,
> Joining the town and just at hand,
> Where waters gushed and fruit-trees grew,
>
> And flowers put forth a fairer hue,...

Of course the sinister implication is that the Piper deceived the children just as he had the rats, but a more optimistic interpretation (and almost certainly an incorrect one) holds that the Piper delivered the children from the hypocritical and dishonest world of Hamelin adults to a perpetual fairy-land where the troubles and hypocrisies of the adult world were always to be kept at bay. In other words, the Piper had been a "catcher" and kept them from "falling".

Title Page Verso[7]

Note the three copyright dates of 1945, 1946 and 1951. Though the novel was published in 1951, portions of it had been printed in magazines prior to that date and copyrighted at the time of publication. *"I'm Crazy"*, an early version of Chapters 1, 21, 22 and 23, was published in the December, 1945 issue of *Collier's* magazine; another story, "Slight Rebellion Off Madison" - which eventually became Chapter 17 - had been sold to *The New Yorker* in September of 1941, but as a result of the Japanese attack on Pearl Harbor and the beginning of World War II its publication was delayed a full five years until December of 1946.

On the book jacket of the first published edition Salinger writes that he "worked on *The Catcher in the Rye*, on and off, for ten years." The truth is that Salinger was only a few years older than his protagonist - Holden is sixteen - when he began to think and write about the young man who would eventually become the protagonist of this novel.

---

[7] Simply put, the word "verso" refers to the other side or back-side of a sheet of paper.

Dedication

"To My Mother"

Not at all unusual. We all had one at one time or another; a mother, that is. Dedicating an enduring work of fiction to one's mother beats the heck out of a corsage or a ceramic figure of a little boy fishing, and goes a long way toward expiating the wrongs of a mischievous childhood.

Salinger's mother, Marie "Miriam" Jillich, an enigmatic figure whose significance in Salinger's life has not been fully explored, died in 1971.

A Note Regarding Dates

I must begin by addressing an on-going controversy. There is some disagreement among reasonable men and women about the precise dates during which Holden experiences the events contained in this novel. It all has to do with how close it actually is to Christmas when Holden decides to leave Pency Prep. Virtually everyone agrees that Holden's trip home has to have occurred on either the weekend of December 10th and 11th or December 17th and 18th, 1949. The year is unquestioned (more about that later).

First, we know that Christmas is coming soon. Holden sees men unloading Christmas trees from a truck. He talks on the telephone to Sally about coming over to trim her Christmas tree. In Chapter 25 he tells us that it is "pretty near Christmas" and he's in an uncharacteristically "Christmasy" mood. At Radio City the "Christmas Spectacular" is in full swing.

Arguments in favor of December 10th go as follows: In Chapter 21 Phoebe tells Holden about a Christmas pageant he is supposed to attend the following Friday. If Holden were visiting Phoebe on Sunday December 18th that would make the next Friday December 23rd, an unusual, though not impossible, date for a school Christmas program. More persuasively, Phoebe also tells Holden that their father is flying to California around that time and will not be able to attend. Unless their father had planned to fly home on Saturday, December 24th his absence for Christmas is both unlikely and uncharacteristic. In addition, the father's unusually rapid turn-around time (24 to 48 hours) in order to be home from California by Christmas would have been a good deal more peculiar for plane travel in 1949 than it would be today.

Arguments in favor of December 17th: For decades it has been customary for American schools to break for a two-week winter recess including both Christmas and New Years Day. That could have been accomplished in 1949 if school recessed on December 16th and resumed on January 2nd. There would have been few good reasons for waiting until December 23rd; it would have pushed forward the resumption of the school calendar to January 9th. (This same set of calendrical circumstances occurred as recently as 2016). Even assuming Phoebe's school had a longer (or shorter) winter recess, it is unlikely that the school board would have waited until December 23 to begin it. In addition, we know that Phoebe attends a private school that conducts field trips on Saturdays, so there should be no reason to assume they operate on the same calendar as public schools. Bottom line: At the time of Holden's visit Phoebe may already have been on her winter break. In support of this theory, the two boys Holden meets in the Museum of Natural History (Chapter 25) tell him that there is no school for them on Monday and this would indicate they are most likely on a winter school recess.[8] In Chapter 17 Sally presses Holden for a response to her invitation to trim the tree with her Christmas Eve. Her urgency suggests that she is not discussing an event a full two weeks in the future.

All in all, and in spite of Mr. Caulfield's ill-timed jaunt to California[9], it does not seem unreasonable that Holden's story should begin on December 17th and conclude on Monday, December 19th, 1949. At least that's the version I prefer and the story I'm sticking with for the time being.

---

[8] Should it matter, Chanukah in 1949 began on December 15th and lasted until December 23rd, and Kwanzaa would not be invented for another eighteen years.
[9] Perhaps he is visiting D.B. or he knows more than Holden thinks he does and is checking out prospective west-coast psychiatric facilities in advance. Or both.

Chapter 1

(Late Saturday afternoon, December 17, 1949)

In which Holden introduces himself and Pencey Prep to readers and visits Mr. Spencer.

> My story is much too sad to be told
> For practically everything leaves me totally cold.
> Cole Porter 1934

Page 1: "...David Copperfield kind of crap..."

David Copperfield, the eponymous hero from Charles Dickens' 18th century novel - not the 20th century illusionist famous for making very large things disappear - tells his life story, beginning with his own birth.

...To begin my life with the beginning of my life, I record that I was born (as I have been informed and believe) on a Friday, at twelve o'clock at night. It was remarked that the clock began to strike, and I began to cry, simultaneously.

In his own first-person narrative Holden, well read as he is, wants the listener to know that he has no intention of reciting all of the details of his life as

Copperfield did. This is as much a result of impatience as it is reluctance to reveal too much about himself.

More often Holden's introductory remarks have been compared to those of Huckleberry Finn, the protagonist of Mark Twain's *The Adventures of Huckleberry Finn* (1885) who begins his own story,

> *You don't know about me without you have read a book by the name of "The Adventures of Tom Sawyer" but that ain't no matter. That book was made by Mr. Mark Twain, and he told the truth, mainly. There was things which he stretched, but mainly he told the truth. That is nothing. I never seen anybody but lied one time or another....*[10]

One crucial difference between the first-person narratives of Huckleberry Finn, David Copperfield and Holden Caulfield is that while David Copperfield and Huckleberry Finn both address the reader directly, Holden is speaking to a third person, most likely a therapist; the reader is, in a sense, eavesdropping. This same device was to work well for Philip Roth nearly twenty years later in *Portnoy's Complaint* (1969).

And as for his parents' concern for their privacy, we'll have to take Holden's word for it. In this novel neither of them gets the chance to tell another side of the story.

Page 1: "hemorrhages":

A hemorrhage results in massive bleeding. Though a hemorrhage can occur virtually anywhere in the body, Holden is referring specifically to a cerebral hemorrhage that is caused by a burst blood vessel in the brain. This typical example of Caulfield hyperbole suggests early on that the story Holden is about to tell is an uncensored, unvarnished and highly

---

[10] I can quote Dickens and Twain at length because their works are in the public domain. Someday *The Catcher in the Rye* will be in the public domain, but don't hold your breath waiting. That day is at least fifty years in the future.

subjective retelling of past events and very likely to annoy or anger some readers.

Page 1: "touchy":

Though modern usage sometimes defines "touchy" as *tending to touch*, what it means to Caulfield and others of this period is *sensitive* or *easily annoyed.*

Page 1: "madman stuff...pretty run-down":

The *mad* in "madman" takes us back to an earlier meaning of the word: *insane*[11]. (This usage still survives in the expressions "mad dog", "madhouse" and "midnight madness".) Holden is referring to something he probably knows, has heard others say, but is reluctant to admit to. His use of "pretty run-down" is a euphemism for what was more likely a psychological crisis or breakdown. In the 1940's and 50's "run-down"[12] covered a wide range or complaints from simple fatigue to pernicious anemia and clinical depression. J.D. Salinger suffered a breakdown of sorts in 1945 following

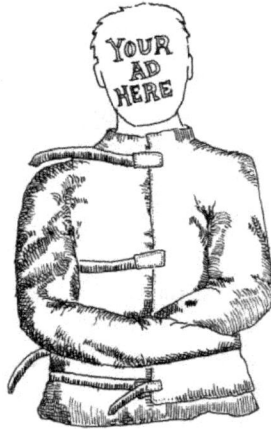

---

[11] Popular synonyms for *mad* include: bats, batty, bugs, buggy, barmy, flipped-out, loony, nuts, nutty, round-the-bend, silly whacked-out, whack-o, and wacky.

[12] In the 40's and 50's a tonic, *Geritol,* was heavily advertised on radio as a remedy for Americans who felt "run-down and listless", particularly those over 50. It was 12% alcohol.

months of military service under combat conditions in Europe. He voluntarily signed himself into an army hospital in Nuremberg, Germany that July He was released in late August after several weeks of care and observation and by September had married the first of his two wives, a French doctor named Sylvia.

The return of a war-traumatized young man to an uncomprehending home was already a common motif by the time *The Catcher in the Rye* was published in 1951. One of Salinger's literary mentors, Ernest Hemingway, wrote about the subject in his stories "Soldier's Home" and "The Big Two-Hearted River". In this respect Holden Caulfield may hold the unique distinction of being the only shell-shocked protagonist who never went to war.

Page 1: "...around Christmas..."

The events around which this story is built all take place in the second or third week of December. Pinning down a year is pretty easy, but problematic. Holden and Sally attend a matinee of "*I Know My Love*" that could only have occurred in 1949. Yet the novel is conspicuously lacking in any other references that would point to the final month in a very tumultuous decade.

The Caulfield family car, we are told, has only recently been equipped with a radio. Notably, no one Holden encounters in his peregrinations ever refers to the phenomenon of television that, by 1949, had already become popular. By the end of that year New Yorkers owned tens of thousands of the video receivers. Surely a family as well off as the Caulfields would have had one. Sally's family would certainly have had one in the living room, why not the Antolinis? Of course, Holden would have been compelled to tell us how much he hated television; but he also tells us how much he despises movies in spite of he fact that he seems to have seen quite a few. The only music Holden seems to be familiar with is pre-World War II. His times seem even more "out of joint" than his precarious mental state would account for and the explanation lies in the discrepancy between Holden's age and Salinger's.

Salinger claims to have first conceived of Holden in 1941 and used the name in stories well before the character had been fleshed out and his personal traits and characteristics consolidated into one character. Some episodes and events in the novel were conceived of in the early 40's. For reasons that will become clear later, many readers have seen Holden as a Sallinger surrogate. The author himself was 16, Holden's age, in 1935. Since nowhere in *The Catcher in the Rye* is there any evidence of or reference to wartime hardships, rationing, shortages or the scarcity of men due to the draft it is possible to imagine that in some ways Holden is operating in a pre-World War II environment. This is altogether fitting since Salinger's own experiences in New York were limited to the years when he was not in Europe fighting the Nazis.

Still, Holden's palpable sense of sorrow, confusion and loss is typical of many post-war protagonists. The few references to late 1940's culture (Olivier's *Hamlet*, S.N. Behrman's *I Know My Love*, D.B.'s wartime service) seem to have been inserted primarily to bring Holden's story into the present day (1950). In a sense it is almost as though Holden missed the war entirely which, since it was single most important event of his life from the ages of eight to eleven, is virtually impossible to imagine. The simplest explanation is that Holden's experiences are essentially pre-war, but have been placed in a post-war setting in an effort to contemporize the story.[13]

Page 1: "D.B.":

Perhaps you have noticed that the brother who is a gifted writer goes by a set of initials instead of a first name much the same as the author of this book. D.B. and Salinger both stormed the

---

[13] A similar situation exists with William Saroyan's *The Human Comedy* (1943). Though ostensibly a story of a closely knit, rural community viewed through the eyes of a boy in central California during the second World War, it is clear to a perceptive reader that the various interrelated stories which make up the novel grow out of Saroyan's childhood recollections of events that took place during World War I.

beaches at Normandy on D-Day as well. It seems that Salinger might have feared from the outset that readers would eventually begin to assume Holden's story was at least semi-autobiographical so he designed D.B. as a decoy. Enough said.

Note: "D.B." rhymes with Phoebe, Holden's sister's name.

Page 1: "Hollywood":

Unless you are reading this in a snow cave above the artic circle you already know all you need to know about the movie capital of the western world. Holden considers Hollywood the last place a real writer ought to find himself.

Salinger, like Holden, hated Hollywood. The one story he sold to the movies, *"Uncle Wiggily in Connecticut"* received the Goldwyn treatment in 1949 (released as "My Foolish Heart" in 1950)[14] and the author was aghast at the result. He never again allowed the movies to ruin one of his stories. It is easy to see how film, a collaborative art form in which many hands work to create a whole, would inevitably frustrate and annoy a reclusive perfectionist. The studios paid writers well, but held their work in low regard

[14] The film starred Dana Andrews and Susan Hayward and was directed by Mark Robson. Trivia mavens will tell you that it features an uncredited appearance (as an extra) by actor/military hero Neville Brand. In World War II Brand was awarded the Silver Star for gallantry in combat, the Purple Heart, the Good Conduct Medal, the American Defense Service Ribbon, the European/African/Middle Eastern Theater Ribbon with three Battle Stars, one Overseas Service Bar, one Service Stripe, and the Combat Infantryman's Badge.

compared to producers, directors and even actors.

Being unable to secure the film rights to *The Catcher in the Rye* has not daunted screenwriters in the least. There have been many films that have tried to capture the essence of Holden's angst on the screen. Three well-known examples are *Rebel Without a Cause* (1955), *The Young Stranger* (1957), and *Ordinary People* (1980) though dozens of others have endeavored to depict a confused young man lost in an unsympathetic urban milieu.

Page 1: "...Hollywood...isn't too far from this crummy place":

The sanatorium or hospital in which Holden is being treated is in Southern California. Salinger may well have had in mind the State Mental Hospital at 1878 South Lewis Road in Camarillo, not far from Ventura. The hospital, now the site of California State University - Channel Islands, closed in 1997, but from 1936 it housed, sheltered and confined thousands of social misfits and the "criminally insane". Jazz saxophonist Charlie "Bird" Parker had been a patient there. A highly controversial process of gradual deinstitutionalization initiated by then Governor Ronald Reagan began sending most inmates home, or to the streets, in the mid-1970's. If Holden was not being cared for at Camarillo the next most likely place would have been the Neuropsychiatric Hospital at the University of California at Los Angeles *(UCLA)*. The UCLA

Neuropsychiatric Hospital is part of a large teaching and research facility on the Westwood (West Los Angeles) Campus. It is, as it has been for decades, a well-staffed autonomous unit capable of dealing with all kinds of mental disorders and conditions. Many patients are encouraged, or required, to participate in live-in therapeutic programs.

Holden's parents may have chosen California for the weather, its remoteness from New York City or on the assumption that doctors on the west coast have extensive experience dealing with nut cases.

Page 1: "...Jaguar...damn near four thousand bucks."

William Lyons' SS Cars Ltd. first introduced the Jaguar motorcar in 1936. In 1948 the D-type racing model XK-120 - which had a top speed of 120 miles per hour - was their sportiest version yet.

No Jaguar of that period could do 200 miles per hour.

Any model of Jaguar today will cost between ten and twenty times the amount D.B. paid.

Page 1: "...The Secret Goldfish..."

One of Salinger's early stories was titled, "A Perfect Day for Bananafish" (*The New Yorker*, 1948). A charming, precocious little girl of about eight or nine (i.e. Phoebe) was a central character. This title, "The Secret Goldfish", is ironic. Since the expression "life in a goldfish bowl" implies that one is constantly observed, what could be secret?

Page 2: "...out in Hollywood...being a prostitute..."

Holden does not want his listener to think that his brother is out on Sunset Boulevard hustling his ass. Holden is trading on the common stereotype of the time which held that one of Hollywood's greatest vices was luring talented writers out west where they squandered their gifts on second and third-rate scripts for moguls whose tastes ran more to schmaltz than real literature. As with most stereotypes, there was more than a grain of truth in this belief. "Great" writers like F. Scott Fitzgerald, William Faulkner and Dasheill Hammet did come to Hollywood to work for the major studios and did, in fact, squander their talents on less-than-worthwhile movie projects. But it can also be said that the studios paid these writers very well and put up with a lot of temperamental nonsense in the process. Spending their studio incomes on too much alcohol didn't help any of these writers, either.

Page 2: "Pencey Prep is...in Agerstown, Pennsylvania."

"Prep" is short for Preparatory School. The image projected to the public was that these expensive, private schools equipped young men and women with the skills and "character" necessary to enter one of the Ivy League Universities upon graduation. Both Pencey Prep and the city of Agerstown,

Pennsylvania are fictional, but because J.D. Salinger had attended *Valley Forge Military Academy* (1934-35) it is thought that he modeled Pencey Prep after that school. As opposed to Holden, J.D. Salinger seems to have enjoyed his prep school years and received welcome attention for his writing and dramatic abilities.

Page 2: "...advertise in about a thousand magazines ...showing some... guy on a horse..."

Commonly, upscale literary magazines that circulated heavily on the east coast like *The New Yorker, Harpers, Scribner's* and *The Atlantic Monthly* ran ads like this (see above) promoting private residential schools. Because polo - a field game where men and/or women on horses knock a ball back and forth across 48,000 square yards of playing field with long sticks – and equestrian sports in general were emblematic of the upper class the ads often included pictures of students engaged in one manifestation or another of dressage. Even if the horse or rider had little to do with the scholastic services offered at the school, the more important message had to do with exclusivity and old money's preoccupation with English tradition.

This ad ran in National Geographic magazine in 1949. Salinger attended Valley Forge Military Academy.

Page 2: "Strictly for the birds."

This is generally obsolete slang meaning both useless and stupid. Something that Holden would have termed "for the birds" might today be called "for losers" or something even more coarse.

Page 2: "...you were supposed to commit suicide or something..."

Holden does not mean this literally. He is again using hyperbole in order to show his disdain for the school spirit all students and alumni are supposed to display at sporting events. However, his use of this phrase and the "...crazy cannon..." which follows touch upon his precarious mental state and foreshadow later events. In fact, see if you can count the

30

number of times Holden uses the words "mad", "crazy", "insane", or a variant of one of those words in the first chapter alone.

Page 2: "...scrawny and faggy on the Saxon Hall side..."

Holden uses the term "faggy" to mean weak and innefectual. "Fag", "faggy", "faggotty" and "fagged" all stem from "faggot". A term that as far back as the 13th century meant a torch or bundle of reeds set aflame. The term later was applied by the English to a cigarette, hard work, the fatigue that results from hard work, a means of harvesting corn with a sickle and a hooked stick, and the younger boys in school who were made to carry out menial and/or exhausting tasks for upperclassmen. By 1350 it wasn't always clear what the terms suggested and to say that someone was a "fagger" could mean that he either had a younger boy running errands for him at school, or was an extremely hard worker. It wasn't until the early 20th century that the term was used to describe homosexuals and more than likely grew out of common knowledge regarding what other kinds of duties those boys were asked to carry out in the English *Public* (read: Private) schools. Since Holden is using this as a term of derision it is quite clear which of these meanings he is relying on and initiates an undercurrent of homophobia that periodically emerges throughout Holden's story.

Page 3: "...damn falsies that point all over the place..."

"Falsies" were lightweight pads that a young lady could wear inside of her brassiere to augment her breasts. In the days before *Wonderbra* and *Victoria's Secret* this was not uncommon. Amanda Wingfield in Tennessee Williams' *The Glass Menagerie* calls them "Gay Deceivers".

While Holden is exaggerating when he says they "point all over the place" - two breasts could do no worse than point in more or less the same direction - it is true that there was a more angular, conical trend in bra-cup design in the late 40's and early 50's and the missile-nose-cone look was not limited to the back end of Cadillacs.

Page 3: "...fencing team...foils..."

En garde, earthling!

Fencing is a collegial and Olympic sport in which the two opponents attempt to score points by sticking each other in strategic spots with long, narrow fighting blades called "foils". Padded, white fencing suits, face guards and gloves were parts of the required equipment. You can learn this at posh academies or private fencing schools, but it is not a part of the curriculum at most public schools in America. In fact, if you were to show up at school wearing a fencing outfit most students would probably think you were some sort of ghost ninja.

In a December, 1949 issue of The New Yorker Magazine, there is a notice of the "Metropolitan Jr. (Fencing) Chapionships at the Saltus Club, YMCA, 215 W. 23rd. St. This competion began at noon on December 17th.

Page 3: "...subway..."

If you live in the U.S. west of the Mississippi River and rarely travel you may never have seen a subway. It is an underground rail system designed to transport commuters to and from their places of work in congested urban environments. Out in the western portion of United States, where land was at least initially cheap and plentiful, cities sprawled and public transportation took place on surface streets or on tracks down the middle of wide thoroughfares.

London, England has the world's oldest subway system (1863) and New York, the city Holden is most familiar with, has had one since 1904.[15] Paris, Tokyo, San Francisco, Madrid and Mexico City have extensive and very busy subway systems.

Subway stations, like the trains and tracks, are built below ground. Commuters enter from street level and descend via stairs or escalators to different levels where they board trains headed toward sequential destinations along a route.

Leaving Manhattan Holden would have taken the subway out of *Pennsylvania Station* (See Chapter 9: "Penn Station") then caught a conventional train back to Agerstown with the rest of the team.

Page 3: "ostracized"

"Cast out" or "banished". From the Greek *ostraka* , literally a shard of pottery on which one registered a vote as to whether or not a guilty individual was to be cast out. Usually social ostracization meant getting the cold shoulder and/or receiving the "silent treatment" from those who had formerly been one's friends.

---

[15] In the musical "On The Town" (1944) the sailors on shore leave sing:
New York, New York, it's a wonderful town!
The Bronx is up and the Battery's down
The people ride in a hole in the ground,
New York, New York, it's a wonderful town!

Page 3: "...the grippe..."

The flu: pronounced "grîp". This term has faded from use in the United States, but survives as "la gripa" in Spanish-speaking countries. Influenza had been a terrible and much-feared disease in the early part of the twentieth century during which there were three serious global epidemics. Hundreds of thousands died in the global pandemic of the "Spanish Flu" in 1918 and 1919, but by the 1940's that was ancient history and the flu was regarded by most as an unpleasant inconvenience rather than a life-threatening tragedy. Modern vaccines have substantially reduced the death toll from periodic outbreaks

Page 4: "...got the axe..."

Literally: killed. Figuratively: fired, dismissed, eliminated or removed from office. The expression stems from the manner in which chickens and geese begin their progress from farmyard to dinner table and European monarchs were officially notified of their redundancy. Other popular metaphors include: "canned", "pink-slipped", and "terminated".

Page 4: "...colder than a witch's teat..."

This is a colorful old expression that unfailingly conjures up vivid sensory images. Salinger did not invent this marvelous simile; the expression goes back at least 250 years to a time when people commonly believed in witches, and given their fondness for late night flying, the extreme frigidity of their mammary glands. In earlier versions the "teat" was often replaced by the word "tit", or another part of the witch's anatomy.

Page 4: "...reversible..."

A lightweight jacket that can be worn inside-out if desired; a windbreaker.

Page 4: "...camel's hair coat..."

A very soft, warm coat of varying lengths and styling which, if genuine, is almost invariably expensive. A camel's hair coat is made from the hair of the double-humped Bactrian camel, and almost always tan in color, though natural variations in shading are common.

Aside from his parents' ability to send Holden to a series of upscale boarding schools, the stolen camel's hair coat is an additional indication that he comes from a family with substantial financial resources.

Page 5: "...Mr. Zambezi..."

The biology teacher has been given the name of one of Africa's fourth largest river systems. Only the Nile, Zaire and Niger Rivers are greater. The Zambezi runs through six countries as it winds from central Africa to the Indian Ocean. It's surging rapids and cataracts have created the awe-inspiring Victoria Falls and the almost impossible-to-navigate Batoka Gorge.

Page 5: "...He lived on Anthony Wayne Avenue..."

Remember when I told you to look for Holden's uses of the words "mad" and "crazy" in this chapter? Here's an oblique one you might otherwise miss. Anthony Wayne, a native of Pennsylvania, was a brigadier general in the American Revolutionary War. Dashing and courageous - as well as quick-tempered - he was known as "Mad" Anthony Wayne for his willingness to charge into the field of battle when more prudent minds urged otherwise.

"Old Spencer" lived on a street named for this colonial-era hero. [16]

Holden would no doubt have been intrigued (or amused) by the fact that "Mad" Anthony Wayne is the only Revolutionary war hero to have two burial sites. Upon his death in 1796 he was interred at Fort Presque Isle, Maine, then in 1809 his brother, convinced that the Brigadier General would have preferred a more southerly burial spot, removed Anthony Wayne's bones - and only the bones; everything else was left behind[17] - and transported them to St. David's Church in Radnor, Pennsylvania.

(See **Chapter 21, Page 162: "Benedict Arnold"**.)

Page 5: "... I practically got t.b...."

Holden is referring to tuberculosis, a disease of the lungs. Whether he ever had it or was in any real danger isn't clear. Obviously something serious took him to the hospital in California, but his problem was more mental and emotional than physical in nature. Given that tuberculosis is one of those things that you either have or you don't and "practically" means *almost*, we can be fairly certain that though Holden was sick he did not have tuberculosis. Holden has an adolescent's fondness for hedging, approximating and exaggerating. Besides, a physical disease with a familiar name can seem less frightening than a mental disorder with a scary one.

---

[16] In Pennsylvania one can also find Waynesburg Borough, the city of Waynesburg, Wayne County, the community of Wayne, the Anthony Wayne Theater, Wayne Township, Wayne Middle School, Anthony Wayne Terrace (housing), General Wayne Elementary School, Waynesburg University and The General Wayne Inn. Oh, and you can also buy yourself a bottle of Mad Anthony Ale.

[17] Well, if you want to know the gruesome details, the bones were boiled to remove any non-bony bits before they were hauled off in a sack. Really. I'm serious.

Page 6: "...I wear a crew cut..."

The "crew cut" was a very short cut mandatory in the Armed forces during W.W.II and popular with civilians throughout the 1950's. It is believed that the "crew" in *crew cut* originally referred to the Yale rowing crew. Virtually any really short hair cut can be called a "crew" whether the wearer bothers to stick it up or not. It differs from the "flat-top" in that the crew cut wasn't generally greased up or planed to a perfect "deck" across the top. By the mid-1960's the crew cut was considered "strictly for the birds" by most young men who were not in the military. (How Holden manages to brush so little hair "back with (his) hand" is not at all clear.)

Chapter 2

(Saturday, December 17, 1949, early evening)

In which Holden visits Mr. Spencer.

> I pray you…
> … take from me
> simple advice: the sooner the better.
> Beowulf, 800 – 1000 M.E.

Page 6: "…half-assed…"

A term still widely used meaning "mediocre" or "executed with little concern or effort". Paradoxically, *whole-assed* would not be an improvement.

Page 7: "…beat-up Navajo blanket…"

The Navajo (Dine') are an Indian nation in the American southwest. For centuries their tribal economy has centered around sheep, textiles and jewelry-making. The Navajo share cultural and ethnic roots with the Apache who speak a related Athapascan language.

Back in the 1940's, before real Navajo blankets had become

costly collector's items and fake Navajo blankets were being knocked off in various Asian Pacific countries, such items were common souvenirs of a trip to the Grand Canyon or Mesa Verde. Yellowstone National Park in Wyoming is, ironically, too far north of the Navajo's home in what is now New Mexico and Arizona to be a good source for authentic Navajo blankets. (For more information look up the hilariously-named *Indian Intercourse Act of 1834*) .

Page 7: "Atlantic Monthly"

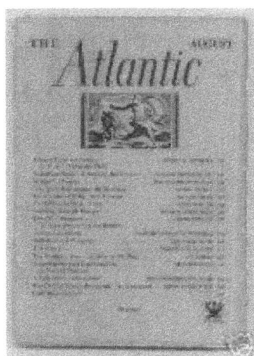

This American literary/ cultural magazine founded in 1857 by James Russell Lowell is still to be found on newsstands. The *Atlantic Monthly* publishes articles on politics and current events with a short story and the occasional poem. Long a New England institution, the publisher surprised thousands by announcing in April of 2005 that their offices would be moved from Boston to Washington, D.C.

Page 7: "...Vicks nose drops..."

Alas, the comforting eucalyptus and menthol scent of *Vicks VapoRub* isn't nearly as common as it used to be in sickrooms around the world, but the *Vicks* brand is still to be found on a wide variety of cold and flu remedies and their cough lozenges are quite popular. The nose drops have been replaced by a spray inhaler.

Page 7: "ratty"

Unacceptably worn-out; old.   Variants include: *raggy*, *raggedy*, *tattered*, *tatty*, and *toe-up*.

Page 8: "...his ass from his elbow..."

To say that someone does not know his "ass from his elbow" is to call him stupid; profoundly ignorant; clueless.   One still hears this from time to time.   Another common variation is "...his ass from a hole in the ground".

Page 8: "...life is a game...

Spencer is speaking metaphorically here and sounding a bit like Polonius (See Chapter 16, page 161: "Ophelia's brother"). Literature is full of well worn metaphors for the passage of life: the winding road, the winding path, the twisting stream, the highway, the play, the struggle, the race, the bowl of cherries, the parade, etc.

"Old Spencer" is not referring to *The Game of Life*, a popular American parlor game played on a colorful board where tiny plastic cars cruise around carrying even tinier plastic families. "*The Game of Life*" was not produced by Milton Bradley (now a subsidiary of Hasbro) until 1960 by which time "old Spencer" would most certainly have been "a goner" (See Chapter 3, Page 46: "stiffs" and Chapter 3, Page 52: "goner").

Page 10: "Five, sir."

Holden had taken five subjects that term at Pencey. He passed English.   He failed history, oral expression (Speech) and biology. Holden doesn't say what the fifth class was, but it was most likely either geometry or trigonometry.

Page 10: "Beowulf"

Beowulf is the oldest known epic poem in a language that can be identified as English. The earliest manuscript version is thought to date to 1000 ME (AD). Dates of composition vary from 8th to 10th century. The story is one of heroic deeds by the protagonist who is called Beowulf (literally "Bear"). His most famous exploits are the hand-to-claw battles with a repulsive creature called Grendel, the monster's *dam* (mother), and a fire-breathing dragon which, sadly - or happily, depending on whether or not you are having a good time reading about it - proves to be his last.

Beowulf's funeral is suitably epic.

While reading the Old English text is impossible for most of us a good translation will provide you with an interesting experience. Irish poet Seamus Heaney has written the most recent, and probably best, translation (2000). Before that the standard was that of Howell D. Chickering. Regardless, if you encounter this in school it will most likely be in an abridged version with some of the more tedious passages excised.[18]

Page 10: "Lord Randal My Son"

This ancient European ballad exists in numerous versions in various languages. An English version is thought to go back as far as the 15th century. It tells the story of a young man poisoned by his lover. When asked by his mother where he is going he replies that he is going to lie down because he is dying - as good a reason as any.

A verse-mystery, "Lord Randal My Son" is a tragedy without a prelude. Consequently, interpretation of this poem poses more than a few questions. Who was Lord Randall, why did his lover wish to see him die, and why does it seem that his mother is somehow implicated in the crime?

---

[18] Rated R for violence, drug use, frequent alliteration and full-frontal kennings.

Page 10: "Whooton School"

Another fictional boarding school Holden attended prior to Pencey Preparatory. Not to be confused with the Wharton School of the University of Pennsylvania.

Page 11: "...ancient race of caucasians..."

Most students are accustomed to the term "caucasian" being synonymous with "white" as a racial designation and find it perplexing to see this label applied to Egyptians who are, of course, north-Africans. However, past usage has included a wide range of peoples who could not otherwise be easily labeled as Negroid or Asiatic, and the application of this term to the Egyptians is meant to establish the belief that they, as a people, migrated down from the north instead of up from the south. Holden's teacher referred to the Egyptians as *caucasian* because the term, until quite recently, was used by physical anthropologists to include a generous slice of the homo sapien pie including many ethnic groups who do not think of themselves as "white".

Page 12: "...ping-pong..."

Originally called "Whiff-Whaff, this game is properly called table tennis. "Ping-Pong" is a trademarked name owned by Parker Bros. Invented in England in the 1880's, this game, played on a broad green table with two paddles and a lightweight cellulose ball, is very popular at summer camp and throughout China. In fact, it is the world's second most popular sport, the most popular being either soccer (football) or Quidditch.

Page 12: "...flunking..."

The use of the word *flunk* to mean *failure or collapse* goes back to at least 1820 and is, as one might expect, of

American coinage.[19]

Page 12: "moron"

"Moron" is an insult meaning "stupid". There was a time when "moron" was a clinical term referring to someone with an IQ between 51 and 70. An "imbecile" had an IQ ranging from 26 to 50 and an "idiot" tested anywhere from 25 on down. Fortunately, these terms have now become the almost exclusive prerogative of precocious grade school children looking for ways to torment each other.

Properly speaking, politicians, runway models and television news anchors should be referred to as "intellectually challenged".

Page 13: "Central Park"

At 842 acres, Central Park in downtown Manhattan is one of the largest and almost certainly the most famous of urban parks in the world. Officially opened in 1856, the park was designed by Frederick Law Olmstead and Calvery Vaux. Its vast acreage contains 36 bridges, several artificial lakes, a zoo, a carousel, dozens of individual sculptures and statues, the *Metropolitan Museum of Art*, a bandshell, a wildlife sanctuary, an ice-skating rink, the Delacorte Theatre and numerous grassy areas and playgrounds.

In 1853, out of desire to create in their city a green sanctuary comparable to the great parks of London and Paris, the City of New York was authorized by the state legislature to acquire

16. Every failure teaches a man something, to wit, that he will probably fail again next time. H.L. (Henry Lewis) Mencken

more than 700 acres of land in the center of Manhattan by means of eminent domain. Turning a vast area of swamp and rocky outcroppings into parkland required the City of New York to evict hundreds of German and Irish immigrants from the shacks and shanties in which they lived. Whole neighborhoods, churches, shops and at least one school ceased to exist. A long-standing African-American neighborhood, Seneca Village, was razed.

By 1857 the city had hired Frederick Law Olmsted to implement his "Greensward Plan" which utilized elements from the English tradition of garden design, a romantic assemblage of natural-looking greenery, meadows, pathways and faux relics of ancient architecture. Walking, riding and carriage paths were to be separated. Calvert Vaux and Jacob Wrey Mould designed more than forty bridges to facilitate crossings. Four Transverse Roads were sunk below the level of the park in order to permit cross-traffic without spoiling the tranquility of the setting.

The realization of Olmstead's plan was one of the most ambitious public works projects of the 19th century. More than 20,000 workers, most of them immigrants, were engaged in the moving of earth, blasting of rock, excavation of tunnels and planting of trees and shrubs. An attractive reservoir was designed and constructed to augment the utilitarian one already in existence. The park opened to the public in the winter of 1859.

Ironically, considering the number of immigrants whose labors had made the park possible, early ordinances and restrictions prevented all but the privileged classes from enjoying it. Children's ball games were discouraged and group picnics forbidden. Tradesmen were not allowed to drive their families through the park in their work wagons. Regulations were particularly strict on Sundays, the only day most working people would have had the time to use the secular sanctuary. It was not until the early decades of the twentieth century that any real democracy governed the standards for use and enjoyment of the park; playgrounds were built, picnic areas designated; game fields set aside. The ugly, rectangular reservoir at the park's center was replaced by the Great Lawn. By the late 1940's, under the leadership of the beloved Mayor Fiorello La Guardia and his (less beloved) parks czar Robert Moses, Central Park had been substantially re-imagined as a place of recreation and amusement for *all* New Yorkers.

If *The Catcher in the Rye* were a play one would expect Acts 2 and 3 to be dominated by a giant cyclorama of Central Park in the winter. The park is so much a part of the story for the last half of the novel that it is virtually a character. Holden first introduces the park in Chapter 9 through a series of questions to his cab driver about the ducks in the pond. In Chapter 25 the novel reaches its climax at the carousel. Between those two chapters Holden walks through, sits in, circles, hovers near and talks about Central Park as though it were a source of sustenance from which he drew strength. More to the point, Central Park is, for Holden, a constant and unvarying symbol of security to which he returns for refuge when his anxieties threaten to overwhelm him.

Most non-New Yorkers know the park best from its frequent appearances in movies and on television. The park comes off especially well in *The World of Henry Orient* (1964), *Manhattan*, *Hair* and *Kramer vs Kramer* (all 1979), and *Angels in America* (2003). Among its scores of supporting roles are appearances in *Annie Hall* (1977), *Carnal Knowledge* (1971), *The Muppets Take Manhattan* (1983), *Marathon Man* (1976), and *On The Town* (1949).

Page 13: "The old bull...shot the bull...shoot the old bull...shooting the bull"

"Shooting the bull" is to engage in conversation of no real importance. It derives from "bullshitting" as a term for talk that is of a boastful nature. Variants include: "shoot the breeze" and "shoot the shit".

Page 13: "Elkton Hills"

Like Whooton, another fictional Prep school Holden has attended.

Page 14: "corny-looking"

Traditionally "corny" has meant *trite* or *dulled by overuse*. A corny joke is stupid, though perhaps still funny. (Old Ossenburger does this in Chapter 3.) A corny movie is full of ideas that have been used in too many other films. By "corny-looking" Holden probably means bourgeois, unfashionable or out of style.

Page 15: "...going through a phase..."

This is a common way of referring to the different periods of development in one's life or the way in which a person moves over time from one set of interests or preoccupations to another. To say that someone is "going through a phase" is to suggest that they are currently displaying a set of behaviors or attitudes that will probably change with time. Sometimes people refer to adolescence as a "phase", when "syndrome" would be more apt.

Chapter 3

(Saturday, late afternoon / early evening)

In which Holden introduces Ackley, the red hunting hat, and Stradlater

> We aren't no thin red 'eroes, nor we aren't no
> blackguards too,
> But single men in barricks, most remarkable like you;
> And if sometimes our conduck isn't all your fancy
> paints,
> Why, single men in barricks don't grow into plaster
> saints.
> Rudyard Kipling, *Barrack-Room Ballads* (1892).

Page 16: "Ossenburger Memorial Wing"

Traditionally schools have rewarded substantial benefactors by naming buildings after them. The name itself is a little joke; roughly translated, *Ossenburger* means "bone-man".

Page 16: "...pot of dough..."

Cash. Money. Dead presidents. Moo-lah.

Page 17: "...stiffs..."

Slang for corpses; dead bodies.

Page 17: "...red hunting hat..."

This is the famous red hunting hat that all Rye-ophiles go nuts over. All in all it is a pretty standard piece of sporting equipment for the time. When Holden refers to the "peak" he is referring to what most of us would call the *bill* or *visor*. This peak is longer than one might find on a baseball cap, but otherwise the hat is built along the same lines. Of course, Holden's hunting cap is probably made of wool, insulated and equipped with fur earflaps that fold down for cold weather wear. The color red was common for hunting hats because it helped well-armed marksmen differentiate between deer and other hunters. (Though the ploy was relatively successful, the red hat never caught on with deer.) Holden doesn't get specific, but it is likely that the hat was made of plaid fabric.

You will frequently hear this hat referred to as an "Elmer Fudd hat" after the Warner Brothers cartoon character often seen "hunting wabbits" and consistently humiliated by Bugs Bunny.

That Holden prefers to wear the hat turned around backwards with the "peak" over his neck is a fairly standard expression of youthful rebellion. Bowery toughs and street kids who would turn their hats sideways or backwards popularized that look back into the 1930's.

L.L. Bean, Cabellas and other outdoor outfitters sell similar hats. A bargain at $1.00; today, if you can find one on ebay, you'll pay a lot more.

Page 18: "Out of Africa"

Danish author Karen Blixen wrote under the pseudonym of Isak Dinesen and later, Pierre Andrezel. She married her cousin, Baron Bror von Blixen-Finecke, in 1914. It was not a good match. He was unfaithful to her and, to make matters worse, gave her syphilis from which she suffered for the rest of her life. Her beautiful memoir of her years on a coffee plantation in Kenya, *Out of Africa*,

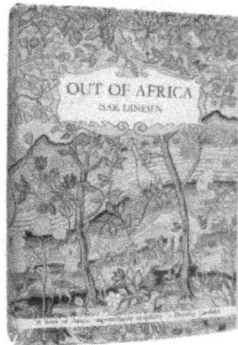

was published in the United States in 1938. Since then it has become a modern classic.

Dinesen's writing was admired by Ernest Hemingway, who was in turn admired by Salinger.

Page 18: Ring Lardner

American journalist, playwright and short story author Ring Lardner (1885-1933) began his literary life as a sportswriter In Indiana. He developed a slangy, breezy style that leaned heavily on the urban vernacular of the 1920's. Eventually he worked his way to Chicago where for many years he wrote a daily column for the *Tribune*. His comic plays were produced on *Broadway* and his short stories entertained readers of the *Saturday Evening Post*. Very popular in his time, he is largely forgotten today because he never wrote a great novel.[20] If you encounter him at all in high school or college it will probably be in a short story anthology where *"Haircut"* and *"The Golden Honeymoon"* are standards. Lardner was one of Salinger's early influences.

Writer/director John Sayles played the part of Lardner in his teriffic baseball film, *Eight Men Out* (1988). The film ably chronicles the

In spite of what this photograph might suggest, Ring Lardner had a terrific sense of humor.

[20] Nevertheless, sportswriters to this day make devoted pilgrimages to his shrine in the Baseball Hall of Fame. He was the second (and no doubt best known) winner of the *J. G. Taylor Spink Award* – Spink himself was the first in 1962 – "for meritorious contributions to baseball writing".

1919 "Black Sox" scandal when several players on the Chicago White Sox conspired to throw the World Series to the Cincinnati Reds.

Lardner's son, Ring Lardner Jr., who was just four years older than Salinger, went on to work in Hollywood and after a difficult and tumultuous career won a Motion Picture Academy Award in 1970 for his screenplay, *"M.A.S.H."*.

Page 18: "The Return of the Native"

One of Thomas Hardy's best novels, *The Return of the Native*, was published in 1878. That Holden would prefer this novel to *Of Human Bondage* isn't surprising. While W. Somerset Maugham and Thomas Hardy were both very much interested in telling compelling stories populated with interesting characters and driven by believable circumstances, the reader never gets the feeling that Maugham is standing at one's shoulder as one gets with Hardy. Also, Hardy's characters populate

Very large mustache with Thomas Hardy attached.

a difficult and uncaring world where their lives are often circumscribed by hardship and tragedy. Hardy had a more intense relationship with his characters and his stories are more expressions of his personality and philosophy of life. Besides, *The Return of the Native* has one of the most attractive and unconventional female protagonists since Emma Bovary and Therese Raquin.

(See "**Eustacia Vye**" below.)

Page 18: "Of Human Bondage"

W. Somerset Maugham in the initial stage of falling sideways to his left

This superb novel by W. Somerset Maugham traces the intellectual and emotional development of the main character, the young Philip Carey, as he travels Europe and encounters men and women who help shape his character. Initially, Philip is naive and torn between two mentors, a romantic Englishman and a more pragmatic American. It is only later, somewhat wiser as a result of his experiences, that he comes to understand the profound differences between pure philosophy and the pragmatism required to negotiate one's life. While Philip's actions are not always admirable and he sometimes behaves cruelly to those around him he is nevertheless sympathetic. 'sound like anyone else we know?

Page 19: "Eustacia Vye"

Eustacia Vye is the sensuous and romantic nineteen year-old bad-girl in Thomas Hardy's *The Return of the Native*. She is what Holden would call a very "sexy" girl. What she really longs for is a man who will sweep her off her feet and take her to exotic places far from the dull-as-gruel heath where she has lived all of her life. Her vital, sensuous nature makes her a sympathetic character, but after causing much trouble for those around her she comes to a tragic end while trying to run away with her lover. Holden returns to the subject of *Eustacia Vye* briefly in Chapter 15 of *The Catcher in the Rye*. [21]

Page 20: "goner"

Slang for someone who is dead, moribund or doomed. Is also often used in a figurative sense to suggest that someone's situation is hopeless.

C'mon, it'll only take a second. There's cake afterwards!

Page 20: "chiffonier"

An old-fashioned term for what most of us would call a chest-of-drawers.

---

[21] (Note: With the exception of *Out of Africa*, which would have been considered "contemporary" by prep school standards, all of Holden's reading falls within the boundaries of standard high school required reading of the time. In spite of stylistic qualities that might at first seem daunting to modern readers, these are all very engaging works. If you can slow your pace down a bit and approximate a more nineteenth century approach to leisure, many of you reading this - and *Catcher in the Rye* - might find them as engaging as Holden did.)

Page 22: "jock strap"

A "jock-strap" is an athletic supporter[22]; a sling of fabric and elastic used to support the male genitals while participating in vigorous physical activity; the focus of an endless gallery of locker-room pranks, jokes and ribaldry.

Page 22: "You got robbed..."

Another way of saying "swindled" or "cheated". Holden does not mean to suggest an assault of any kind.

Page 22: "...a people shooting hat...I shoot people in this hat."

"*Catcher*" analysts and literary exegesists have sometimes used this quote to suggest latent homicidal tendencies in Holden. While I am willing to admit that Holden may carry around some repressed anger I do not believe there is any subconscious threat or foreshadowing implied by this remark. Holden's whole manner of dealing with Ackley is sarcastic and facetious. This is just another wisecrack.

Page 23: "...wooden press..."

Back in the days when all tennis rackets were made from laminated wood it was common to store them in protective wooden frames. These frames, which generally had tightening bolts with wing-nuts on each of four corners, held the racquet face rigid and helped to prevent bending and warping due to temperature/humidity changes. The frame would have more

---

than tripled the weight of the racket and made it a very unpleasant object to be hit by.

Page 23: "...horny-looking..."

Here Holden is using the word "horny" in its literal sense to mean hard and rough. Today the word usually suggests a state of sexual arousal, but Holden prefers to use the word "sexy" for that sense. (See Chapter 4: "sexy bastard".)

Page 23: "...sonuvabitch..."

This compound noun is a phonetic respelling of "son of a bitch"; an insult, unless you are a puppy, in which case "whelp of a bitch" would be more correct. This term is not to be tossed-about lightly; improper use could result in a beating.

Page 25: "...hound's-tooth jacket..."

A once-common pattern in woven fabrics in which jagged edged parallelograms of contrasting shades and colors appear in a tessellated motif. Has nothing to do with "sonuvabitch", "puppy" or "booze hound".

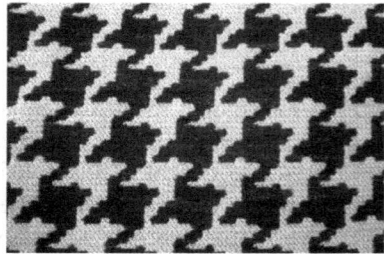

Chapter 4

(Saturday, early evening)

In which Holden and Stradlater fight.

> When he talks he is seeking
> Words to get off his chest.
> Horizontally speaking
> He's at his very best.
> Lorenz Hart. 1940

Page 26: "...chewed the rag..."

To have a conversation; to talk with someone, usually inconsequential. Also commonly heard as "chew the fat" or "shoot the breeze". (See **Chapter 8, Page 55:"...shooting the old crap...".**)

Page 27: "Song of India"

Paul Whiteman had a big hit with this composition in 1921. Tommy Dorsey recorded it twice and had top ten hits in both 1936 and 1943. The song is based on the dramatic aria *"Chanson Indoue "* from Rimsky-Korsakov's 1897 opera, *Sadko*. The melody would be quite familiar to most people over 50 years of age, but it is unlikely you have ever heard it except in an elevator or a dentist's waiting room.

Page 27: "Slaughter on Tenth Avenue"

This is both the name of the show-within-a-show and the main balletic set piece in *"On Your Toes"* (1936) by Richard Rogers with book and lyrics by Moss Hart.[23] For its time, "Slaughter on Tenth Avenue" was an ambitious instrumental composition for the stage that in tone and color was influenced by the work of George Gershwin in the late 1920's, especially "Rhapsody in Blue". The many changes in mood, rhythm and tone would make the entire composition about as difficult to whistle as Stravinsky's "Rite of Spring". If Stradlatter was going to make a mess out of any tune it would be this one.

"On Your Toes" might best be described as a farce *en point*. Its characters include gangsters, ballet dancers and vaudeville [24] acts. Junior, a youthful stage performer-turned-music-teacher, writes a jazz ballet which he is eager to sell to a Russian touring company. Despite a love triangle involving Junior, an eager coed and the prima ballerina, "Slaughter on Tenth Avenue" is the show that must go on. Finally, through a series of improbable events, Junior ends up dancing the lead in the ballet while gangsters - who have mistaken him for someone who owes them money - shoot at him from the audience. (Holden will return to this gangster/gunshots motif in later chapters.) The stage production was directed by George Abbott and choreographed by George Balanchine both of whom would go on to become Broadway legends.

---

[23] Interestingly, the original production starred Roy Bolger and Tamara Geva (Gevergeyeva). Ballerina/actor/singer Tamara Geva (often billed as just "Tamara") first sang the classic song "Smoke get in Your Eyes" in the operetta Roberta in 1933. See note below: **Page 211: "Smoke Gets in Your Eyes"**

[24] "Vaudeville" is the term used to describe a very popular form of variety programming which played in theaters all over the United States from the turn of the century to the early 1950's. On any given night one might be able to see jugglers, comics, scenes from Shakespeare, trained dogs, classical violinists, clowns and tap dancers all sharing the same stage. Television pretty much killed it, though video variety programs of the 1950's and 60's employed many of the same acts.

As you read on in *Catcher in the Rye* you will see how comments Holden makes later tie in with his awareness of many of the corny dramatic conventions "On Your Toes" was intended to satirize.

Page 27: "...up the creek..."

In a very difficult predicament; in trouble. A shortened version of the saying, "up the creek without a paddle". Sometimes, "...up shit creek..."

Page 29: "Ziegfeld Follies"

For almost 40 years the Ziegfeld Follies was shorthand for extravagant, sexy entertainment. Florenz Ziegfeld, Jr. was an impresario whose genius was in hiring the most talented performers in the world and presenting them in a glamorously staged context.

Born in Chicago in 1867, Florenz Ziegfeld, Jr. first gained notoriety presenting "Sandor" a beautifully-sculpted strong man at the Chicago World's Fair. His career really took off when he was able to sign Anna Held, a charming and talented European singer, to an exclusive contract. Looking to create an entertaining revue along the lines of the French *Follies Bergere* Ziegfeld called his show *Follies of the Day*. Ziegfeld wanted to dazzle his audience with an eye-popping amalgam of stupendous glamour, comedy and, of course, girls wearing as little as possible given the standards of the day. After its success New York, the first *Follies* went on a brief tour.

"Flo", as friends called him, always insisted on hiring top-notch talent that over the course of many years included Bert Williams, the first African-American to be integrated into what had been up to then an exclusively "white" show, Fanny Brice, Billie Burke (Who became Ziegfeld's last in a series of wives), singer Eddie Cantor, acrobat/comic W.C. Fields and cowboy humorist Will Rogers. Ziegfeld's last major production was the musical stage play *Show Boat* (1927) from Edna Ferber's popular novel with music by Jerome Kern and lyrics by Oscar Hammerstein II. *Show Boat* quite literally changed the course of American musical theatre and has continued to be one of the most popular and enduring musicals ever written for the American stage.

The years of the Great Depression (1929 to the early 1940's) were as hard on New York theatre owners and producers as anyone else. Money was hard to come by and, with what little they had, most Americans had more pressing needs to address than attending the theater. Ziegfeld's extravagant lifestyle took its toll on his already precarious financial status. He died 1932.

Page 30: "...half nelson..."

Contrary to what Holden believes, a half nelson is not a choke hold. It is a wrestling hold where one combatant's right (or left) arm slides underneath the opponent's right (or left) arm from behind. The hand is then placed behind the head of the opponent and leveraged forward. It is painful and makes it hard for the opponent to escape, but it does not cut off his air supply. A full nelson is basically the same as described above but performed with both arms. If somebody gets you into a full nelson you're probably a "goner".

Page 31: "...B.M...."

Ten miles west of Philadelphia, Bryn Mawr College was named after the Welsh home of its founder. Established in 1885, the name "Bryn Mawr" means "large hill" in Welsh. Originally Quaker, it has been nondenominational since 1893. It is one of the Seven Sisters Colleges. Interestingly, the college's 135-acre campus was designed by Frederick Law Olmsted and Calvert Vaux who also designed Manhattan's Central Park.

Also a joke: A "BM" is euphemistic code for *bowel movement*, which itself is a euphemism for the act of excreting feces.

Page 31: "Shipley"

Shipley is a kindergarten through 12th grade comprehensive school located on the Bryn Mawr campus. It was founded in 1894 to help prepare students for entrance to Bryn Mawr.

Page 31: "Vitalis"

A popular men's hair dressing of the 50's, it is still available, though not nearly as popular as it once was. Not to be confused with a popular brand of German condoms or the 7th century African saint who was burned alive, *Vitalis* is an amber/yellow alcohol-based liquid which was splashed on the hands and rubbed through the hair before combing. It carried with it a masculine perfume that to men of an older generation is still suggestive of barbershops, fraternal orders and a boisterous uncle who never married and drove a sports car.

Vitalis has been immortalized in a lyric from *Guys and Dolls* (1950) by Frank Loesser.

> *When a lazy slob takes a goody steady job,*
> *And he smells from Vitalis and Barbasol.*[25]

---

[25] The brand name of a shaving cream.

Call it dumb, call it clever
Ah, but you can get odds forever
That the guy's only doing it for some doll.

Page 32: "caddy"

If you've got the bucks, this is the guy who will carry your golf clubs around for you while you walk the greens. On the professional level caddies provide more sophisticated services and command good salaries, but in past decades it used to be a good weekend/summer job for high school and college-age boys.

Page 32: "...a hundred and seventy, for nine holes..."

Or, roughly an average of eighteen strokes per hole; very bad golf. This is probably another of Holden's flights of hyperbole.

Page 32: "booze hound"

Someone who drinks too much. "Booze" is any kind of alcoholic beverage. The hound is a dog breed known for sniffing out what it is after regardless of how well it may be hidden. The hound, and dogs in general, have become symbolic of persistence, hence the terms *hound-dog, hounded, bird-dog, wolf* and the adjective *"dogged"*. Dogs, of course, are virtually synonymous with human males.[26]

In 1953 Big Mama Thornton first recorded the blues song, "Hound Dog", but Elvis Presley had a bigger hit with more or less the same song in 1956.

Page 32: "sexy bastard"

---

[26] I can't imagine why.

What Holden really means is that Stradlater is preoccupied with sex, but the ambiguity of the phrase has led to other interpretations by those who believe that one of Holden's problems is his discomfort with - or fear of - his own sexuality.

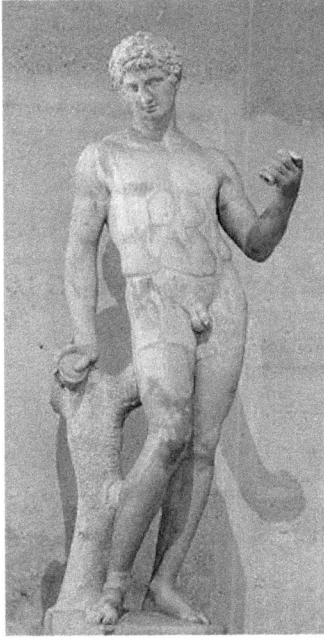

Adonis, (who else?)

Slang terms for someone who has sex on his mind vary from one era to another and include "horny", "randy", "sprung", "sex-crazed", etc. To describe someone as "sexy" generally implies that that person is attractive, and desirable. While Holden pretty clearly does not intend that meaning when he is talking about Stradlatter, there is plenty of evidence to suggest that he does find Stradlatter attractive. We are told how "*very* handsome" Stradlater is. Holden is quite conscious of his "very broad shoulders", "heavy beard" and "damn good build". So, when Holden calls Stradlater a "sexy bastard" students of Freudian[27] psychology may read much more into his comment than

Holden intends to reveal

Page 33: "...heat in the can..."

"Can" is a slang term for bathroom or toilet. The term has always been popular in the Navy.

---

[27] Followers of *Sigmund Freud*, the "father of psychiatry" (1856-1939) believe that people often reveal their hidden feelings through little mistakes in their speech, hence the term "Freudian slip".

Page 34: "muffler"

A muffler is a scarf, usually wool, worn around the neck in cold weather.

Page 34: "...signed out for nine-thirty..."

Jane had to sign in and out of her dormitory. Close watch was kept on girls who lived away from home and there were harsh penalties - up to and including expulsion - for returning late from an outing. Parents were paying good money to send their daughters away to school and needed reassurance that the girls were being held to a high standard of moral propriety. (No doubt the policy also allowed girls a handy excuse in the event that a date was not going well.) As recently as the early 1970's this practice was still common on many private college campuses. I suppose there are still places where the custom is observed, but with the advent of coed dorms in the early 1970's the whole thing began to seem pretty pointless.

Page 35: "handkerchief"

A lightweight piece of cotton fabric carried by men and women for wiping their noses, soaking up perspiration, dabbing at tears or maintaining the cleanliness of children's ears. Not to be confused with a *bandanna* which looks similar but serves a wider range of purposes for cowboys, gay cruisers[28] and urban gangsters. Slang terms for *handkerchief* include "hankie", "snot-rag" and "booger-bagger".

---

[28] During the 1960's and 70's gay men in New York and San Francisco developed an elaborate bandanna code which was used to advertise availability and communicate preferences. The color of the bandanna along with which of the two rear pockets it emerged provided all of the information a prospective partner might need to determine what sort of sex activity the wearer preferred.

Chapter 5

(Saturday evening)

In which Holden goes into Agerstown with Brossard and Ackley. Allie and his baseball mit are introduced.

> ...For why
> Will man lament the state he should envy?
> To have so soon 'scaped world's and flesh's rage,
> And if no other misery, yet age!
> Rest in soft peace...[29]
> Ben Jonson, 1603

Page 35: "Brown Betty"

"Brown Betty" or "Apple Brown Betty" is a dessert of spiced apples baked under a layer of bread crumbs, cinnamon, brown sugar and butter. When properly prepared it has a crisp, sweet-buttery crust covering a moist apple filling. It is frequently served with ice cream, custard or vanilla sauce on top. Holden obviously does not hold this dish in high regard, but I'll bet you'd like it if you had some.

---

[29] Ben Jonson's "On My First Son" memorializes a child who died in infancy.

Page 35: "...horsing around..."

In this context, "horsing around" means playing roughly and/or noisily. Also called "horse play". A term derived from the frolicking of colts in a pasture.

(See **Chapter 17, Page 180 "...horsed around..."**)

Page 36: "...lousy..."

"Lousy" literally means infested with lice, but in modern times it has been used to describe anything the speaker doesn't like. A common insult, it can mean cheap, worthless, cruel, dangerous, rude, thoughtless, inept, awkward or foul smelling.

Page 36: "galoshes"

These are rubber overshoes worn in rainy or snowy conditions. In England they are still called *wellies* (a shortening of *Wellington boots*) or "gum boots", and up until W.W. II Americans commonly referred to them as "rubbers[30]", a word which never fails to elicit amused confusion when students read the poem *"One Wants a Teller in a Time Like This "* by Gwendolyn Brooks.

> *"...Put on your rubbers and you won't catch a cold*
> *Here's hell, there's heaven.*
> *Go to Sunday School..."*

Page 37: "pinball machine"

Back in the days before electronic games and smartphones, people used to go to arcades, bars, bowling alleys and pool parlors to stand and frustrate themselves before a large, garish console called a pinball machine. After inserting the requisite number of coins the player would, with his right hand, propel

---

[30] In modern American parlance "rubbers" refers almost exclusively to condoms.

a steel ball into the glass covered play area where it bounced off of, though and between "bumpers" as it careened back and forth down an inclined surface. There were sound effects to accompany each hit. Depending on how the ball progressed through its travels one would earn points to win free games and/ or prizes.

Page 37: "Cary Grant"

A British-born American actor (1904-1986) known for his slick good looks and debonaire charm. Adept at both comedy and drama, his career lasted for more than 34 years. Great Cary Grant movies include: *Bringing Up Baby* (1938), *Gunga Din* (1939), *His Girl Friday* (1940), *Mr. Blandings Builds His Dream House* (1948), *Monkey Business* (1952) and *North by Northwest* (1959)

Page 37: "bridge"

A popular and card game played with a standard 52-card deck. This game has been around in several forms for at least 400 years and is essentially a variation on the earlier game of *whist*. The game we call *Bridge* today is properly known as *Contract Bridge* and while devotees keep predicting its renaissance you're unlikely to find anyone under the age of fifty playing it.[31]

---

[31] Well, at least as of the early 21st century.

Page 37: "boardwalk"

In the late 19th century, beach resorts sprang up along the east coast from New Jersey south. Since tourists in those days took their seaside strolls fully dressed with shoes and stockings, one common way to provide resort clients with convenient access to sea air was a raised sidewalk made of wood. Planks were nailed above supporting trestles and came to be called "boardwalks". Atlantic City had the most famous of these boardwalks. In some parts of the country they have been maintained and are still used by tourists.

Page 38: "...my brother Allie..."

Allie's death and its impact on Holden are at the fulcrum of the novel's dramatic thrust. Holden is consumed with sorrow and guilt over his brother's death from leukemia. Most of what is troubling Holden can be traced back to Allie's death in Maine in July of 1946. That Allie's death coincided with the beginning of Holden's adolescence heightens the pervading sense of loss and confusion that permeates the novel.

It may be argued that, on a symbolic level, Allie and Holden are simply different representations of the same person. The idealized Allie is who Holden was before he lost his "purity", and Holden, lost and all but purposeless, is the end result of the corrupting influences of time and circumstance.

On a more perfunctory level, Allie's death helps to place the time of the story to somewhere between 1948 and 50.

Page 38: "red hair"

Historically, red hair was considered an indicator of a quick temper and rash behavior. Holden would like his listener to know that this was not the case with Allie.

Much has been made of the fact that Holden's hat and Allie's hair are both red.

In Scotland, 13% of the population has red hair. The percentage of redheads in the U.S. is said to be somewhere between 4% and 6%.

Page 39: "typewriter...jamming"

Once upon a time, whenever someone wanted to create a document that would look as much as possible like a printed page it was necessary to use a mechanical device known as a typewriter. The typewriter was a metal console about the size of a computer printer. A tiered keyboard arranged very much like that of a computer faced the user. Each key on the keyboard was attached by a series of levers to an arm inside the machine that ended in a letter of the alphabet, both upper and lower case. Striking one of the mechanical keys with a finger would force the arm inside the typewriter upward in much the same way as a piano key strikes a note. A sheet of paper was inserted at the top and wound around a *platen,* a hard rubber-coated cylinder, which exposed only a portion of the sheet to the striking surface of the key. As the key struck the surface of the paper, an inked ribbon shot up briefly between the paper and the face of the key and caused the raised surface to leave a black, or occasionally red, impression behind along with a satisfying "thwack".

The result looked a lot like this.

When the end of a line of text was reached the typist heard a tiny bell "ding" and knew it was time to throw the return arm, a chromed lever at the left-hand side of the platen, which rotated the paper slightly upward and brought the sheet from the far right margin to the far left where a new line would begin.

Certainly one of the biggest drawbacks to typewriters was that corrections could only be made with an eraser or a cover-up film or liquid. More substantial editing required that the entire document be retyped. Also, if more than one copy of a document was required it became necessary to insert *carbon paper*[32] between each sheet of paper. The carbon paper transmitted a second inked impression of the typed text to the sheet of paper behind it.

"Jamming" was a common problem for less-skilled typists. It occurred when two or more keys were pressed simultaneously or in too rapid succession and got stuck together mid-way. You had to reach inside with your finger and break up the jam.

Early typewriters were bulky, heavy affairs made of steel. In the 1920's and 30's typewriters became increasingly smaller and lighter enabling the users to carry them from place to place in protective cases with handles. Ironically, near the end of the typewriter's era IBM was producing electronic models that were heavier and bulkier than the earliest 19th century models.

Literary icon Mark Twain is considered to be the first important American author to use a typewriter to compose manuscripts.

The typewriter was at once complicated and elegantly simple. They were the secretary's workhorse from about 1870 until the advent of the word-processor/PC in the late-1970's. Well into the 1980's typewriters were still widely used by students and writers. Today, aside from nostalgic wordsmiths who early in life fell in love with the sounds, and "feel" of mechanical keys, typewriters are curiosities confined to closets and museums. You can usually find several for sale on ebay.

Page 39: "sinus"

A *sinus* is any cavity in the skull. They have evolved for various reasons but their primary benefits are improved ventilation of the brain, facilitated circulation of blood and reduced of head

---

[32] A thin sheet of tissue inked on one side so that when placed between two sheets of typing paper would create a second image behind the original typed letter.

weight. The sinuses most familiar to us are those behind the nose and eyes where congestion can cause headache pain.

LOSE BAD BREATH - keep your friends

In spite of all that has been written about bad breath, thousands still lose friends through this unpleasant fault. Yet sour stomach with its resultant bad breath is frequently only the result of constipation. Just as loss of appetite, early weakness, nervousness, mental dullness, can all be caused by it.

So keep regular. And if you need to assist Nature, use Dr. Edwards' Olive Tablets. This mild laxative brings relief, yet is always gentle. Extremely important, too, *is the mild stimulation it gives the flow of bile from the liver, without the discomfort of drastic, irritating drugs.* That's why millions use Olive Tablets yearly. At your druggists, 15¢, 30¢, 60¢.

"Thousands will lose friends due to this unpleasant fault."

Page 39: "halitosis"

A medical term for bad breath. (Isn't it interesting that most medical terms are for things you'd rather not have?)

Chapter 6

(Saturday night after nine pm)

In which Holden and Stradlater negotiate conflicts.

> "With my hands I will not fight for the girl's sake,
> Neither with you nor any other man...
> > *The Illiad*, Homer
> > (Lattimore translation), 800 BME

Page 40: "...I even have to go to the bathroom when I worry...(o)nly, I don't go."

The inability to urinate even when you want to is called *paruresis*. For most sufferers it is a social phobia arising from the presence of others in a public restroom, though that doesn't seem to be Holden's problem. To help understand Holden's particular difficulty you might wish to consult an expert.

According to *my.webmd.com*:

> *While some paruretics trace their first symptoms to emotional, physical, or sexual abuse, and others to a particularly anxiety-provoking toilet training experience, the vast majority blame a specific, traumatic event in early adolescence.*

Page 41: "...stroking his stomach or his chest..."

While certainly an indicator of narcissism, the behavior Stradlater is exhibiting marks a regression to an infantile state. In babies, self-stimulation is calming and reassuring. For various reasons some children carry these and similar behaviors well into adolescence.

> *Some babies who are left alone too much to entertain themselves will use self-stimulation to compensate for not enough intimate pleasurable person-to person interactions with caregivers. They may masturbate...as a sign that they need their precious parents and caregivers to help them toward more secure feelings of being lovable.*
>
> Alice Sterling Honig, Ph.D.
> http://www.scholastic.com/earlylearner

> *Children (touch) themselves...as a form of self-stimulation. In its natural form, such behaviour is usually self-soothing and is readily amenable to inhibition placed on the behaviour in the form of parental or societal restrictions: children readily learn that they are not supposed to touch themselves in public and thus inhibit the behaviour in public.* [33]
>
> Consulting Psychology Associates, Inc.
> http://www.consulting-psych.com/

Page 41: "backasswards"

To complete a task badly, whether through incompetence or malice is an *ass-backward* piece of work. Stradlater's corruption of the term as "backasswards" is not unique. (I first became acquainted with this term while working my way through college in a refrigeration compressor warehouse. My

---

[33] Which is to say, it feels good and we'd all be doing a lot more of it if people didn't look as us strangely when we did.

supervisor was inclined to use it fromt time to time in spontaneous oral evaluations of my performance.)

Page 42: "...give her my regards..."

The same as "give her my best wishes" or "tell her I said hello". This is one of those oddly formal verbal expressions that seems so out of place in the context of Holden's overall brash vernacular. What it tells us is that at one time Holden was a polite little boy whose parents taught him what were then termed "the social graces".

Page 43: "...pets..."

The term "teacher's pet" is a traditional schoolyard taunt that brands the target as a classroom favorite who is believed to receive special favors and consideration. The utterance of this epithet is generally followed by the impact of a damp glob on the back of the alleged "pet's" head or, worse, a rough thrust initiating a somersault down a steep flight of stairs.

Oddly, it is almost never a compliment.

Page 43: "Give her the time…"

This is certainly one of the strangest and most memorable of Holden's euphemisms. What he means, of course, is "sexual intercourse" (as he makes clear in Chapter 7), but how giving someone "the time" came to mean "sex" is not at all clear.

Giving someone "the time" generally demonstrated a willingness to help out, and expressed in the negative, a metaphor for expending as little effort as possible, i.e. "I

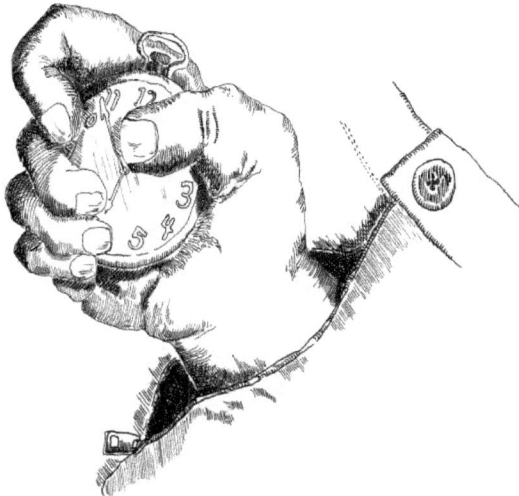

wouldn't give him (or her) the time of day", or "He's not worth the time…". As near as I can tell it appears that the expression as Holden intends it is unique to this novel. There are three realistic possibilities:

1. Salinger invented it, perhap at the suggestion of an editor, to replace a coarser expression

2. Salinger first ran across this terminology in prep school where it was adopted by a small group of boys who all knew each other - coded speech, as it were;

3. Salinger heard it in the army. (Does it sound like G.I. talk to you? Me neither.)

Of the three choices I'm inclined to go with the second explanation.

Chapter 7

(Saturday night after 11:00)

In which Holden frets over Stradlater's date, asks Ackley about life in a monastery, and leaves Pencey Prep.

> Ne that a monk, whan he is recchelees,
> Is likned til a fissh that is waterlees,-
> This is to seyn, a monk out of his cloystre
> But thilke text heeld he nat worth an oystre;
> And I seyde his opinioun was good.
> What sholde he studie, and make hymselven wood
> Upon a book in cloystre alwey to poure(?) [34]
> > Geoffrey Chaucer,
> > Prologue to *The Canterbury Tales*, 1400

Page 47: "canasta"

A popular card game that originated in South America at the beginning of the twentieth century. The word *canasta* is Spanish for *basket* and refers to the pot of cards in the center of the table between the players. It is generally a four-person game, but apparently Ackley knows a two-man variation.

---

[34] No, you haven't gone dyslexic, this text is in Middle English and reads like this:
(It has been said) that a lazy monk
is much like a fish out of water –
that is, a monk out of his cloister.
But (our friend) thought that belief was stupid,
And I agree.
Why should he study until he's gone nuts
From reading books all day in his cell?

What with television, VDR's, P.C.'s, ipod's, DVD's, smartphones, etc. people just don't play card games much any more. In the late forties and early fifties, however, there was a real craze for card games and inviting friends over for games like bridge, canasta, penochle, whist, poker, euchre or mah jong (played with tiles, but essentially a card game in all other respects) was considered both fun and stylish.

Page 47: "Ely"

Poor Ely. He could have been a character in a famous novel if he'd just stayed at school this one weekend.

Remember: Timing is everything. Too soon and you're an interruption; too late and you're a footnote.

Pages 47 and 48: "You're a real prince. You're a gentleman and a scholar..."

That is, "you're a fine man!". Holden is, of course, being sarcastic. This is a variation on an old, elaborate way of praising someone's character. The full version, as I have heard it, goes: *"You are a gentleman and a scholar and a judge of good whiskey"*. There are myriad variations on this phrase. Often "horses" or "cigars" is substituted for "whiskey".

Page 49: "snowing"

Telling someone a lot of nonsense to flatter, confuse or deceive them is often referred to as a "snow job". As the metaphor suggests, the recipient of this treatment finds himself (or herself) so thoroughly buried in semantic "snow" that they are at least temporarily disoriented. When you "snow" someone you are lying with the intent of gaining something.

In common parlance "Bullshit" or "Bullshitting" is completely interchangeable with "snow" and "snowing".

Page 50: "You're aces"

More sarcasm. The phrase means: You're the best; you're a prince; you da man!

Page 51: "Kolynos toothpaste"

A brand of toothpaste advertised on the radio in the 1940's. Kolynos toothpaste and powder was a sponsor of the program, *"Mr. Keen, Tracer of Lost Persons"*. Announcer Larry Elliot promoted its ability to shine teeth "better than jeweler's polish" without leaving a gritty feeling in the mouth. How is this possible? Well, the polishing agents in Kolynos were ground "superfine" to clean teeth and freshen your breath, both of which we were reminded were essential to popularity and success.

The brand name is still owned by Colgate-Palmolive, but is marketed primarily in Latin America where the bulk of its sales are in Brazil (and explains those blindingly radiant smiles).

You Can Choose Kolynos* With Confidence

ACCEPTED for advertising by the AMERICAN DENTAL ASSOCIATION

Kolynos—with extra cleaning action— and kids love it!

2 GIANT TUBES

Page 51: "Gladstones"

A type of suitcase with flexible, leather or fabric sides built around a rigid frame. Named for British Liberal party statesman

and Prime Minister William Ewart Gladstone (1809 – 1898). He was a political reformer who rarely saw eye-to-eye with Queen Victoria. Politicians and the general public regarded him highly for his stirring speeches. For many years he was the Liberal party representative most capable of facing off against the formidable Benjamin Disraeli. One characteristically quixotic crusade that would have endeared him to Holden was his advocacy for London prostitutes. When not speaking out for the creation of institutions for their rehabilitation, he would frequent their gathering places and urge them to change their ways.

Page 52: "Spaulding's"

Spauldings was a chain of department stores in the northeastern states. Not to be confused with *Spalding* sporting goods.

Page 52: "all her marbles"

Holden's grandmother is approaching senility. She's not playing with a full deck; not driving on all six cylinders; one crayon short of a box; one egg short of a dozen; one sandwich short of a picnic; not the sharpest knife in the drawer; no light on upstairs. Grandma is not of sound mind.

Page 52: "Sleep tight..."

This is a very old fashioned way of wishing someone a good night.

"Good night, sleep tight, don't let the bedbugs bite" is the extended version. The Oxford English Dictionary tells us that at one time the adverb "tightly" meant '*effectively*, *thoroughly*, or *soundly*', consequently the expression to "sleep tight' was simply a blessing that one sleep soundly through the night.

A Catcher's Companion

Chapter 8

(Saturday around midnight, December 17/18, 1949)

In which Holden encounters Ernest Morrow's mother on the way to Penn Station.

> This train don't pull no jokers, this train
> This train don't pull no sleepers
> don't pull nothin' but the righteous
> people, this train.
> Gospel folk tune

Page 53: "station"

Train station. Holden is boarding at a small commuter train station in Pennsylvania where one of the many lines that feeds into New York has a stop. If Pency Preparatory is modeled after Valley Forge Military Academy, then Holden would have taken the line from Philadelphia (Agerstown) to Trenton, New Jersey where Ernest Morrow's mother boarded.

Page 53: "...earlaps..."

Earlaps or "earflaps", as some would call them, are fur or fleece ear covers attached to the hat that the wearer can fold down when the weather gets really cold (see illustration on page 48). These flaps were generally either half-ovals, sometimes tied at the top, which folded directly down from the sides of the hat, or part of a broad band which lowered to warm both the back of the neck and the ears. In any event Holden's hat was not what is called a "deerstalker". The deerstalker, favored by Sir Arthur Conan Doyle's famous detective Sherlock Holmes, had a short bill protruding from both the front and the back. Its earflaps were characteristically tied up at the crown.

Page 53: "dumb stories in a magazine"

From the early 19th century into the 1950's there were dozens of monthly magazines that devoted at least a portion of each issue to short fiction. Some of the most familiar were *Colliers, Scribners, The Saturday Evening Post, Cosmopolitan, Seventeen, Harper's, Esquire, Story, The Atlantic Monthly, Cosmopolitan, The New Yorker, Good Housekeeping* and (from 1950 on) *Playboy*. These magazines published short fiction by the best American authors. Writers like F. Scott Fitzgerald, Ernest Hemingway, Willa Cather, John Steinbeck, Katherine Mansfield, John Updike, Irwin Shaw and Philip Roth saw their earliest – and in many cases, best - work published in this way. While some of these magazines are still published, few continue to feature works of short fiction.

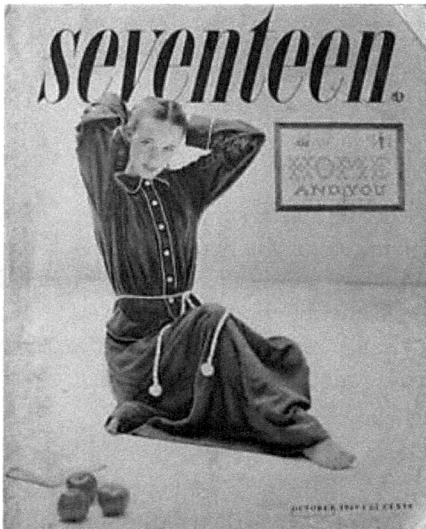

Of lesser renown were countless other magazines aimed primarily at younger female readers which routinely published the kind of formulaic drivel Holden is ridiculing here. Think of *The Homemaker's Companion*, the magazine that Amanda Wingfield peddles over the phone in Tennessee Williams' *The Glass Menagerie*: "I knew that you wouldn't want to miss out on the wonderful new serial...by Bessie Mae Hopper, the first thing she's written since *Honeymoon for Three."*. Often these corny melodramas (or bittersweet romances) were penned by hacks who eked out a living cratfting cookie-cutter tales for an indiscriminate audience, but from time to time first-rate authors wrote for these magazines – exemplified by the enduring bond between F. Scott Fitzgerald and *The Saturday Evening Post* - simply because they paid well and even artists need to eat – or, in Fitzgerald's case, drink.

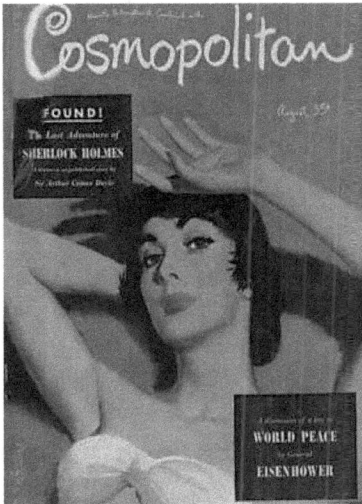

On another level Holden's comment may be taken as a kind of "in-joke". These same magazines that Holden disparages published much of J.D. Salinger's early short fiction.

Page 54: "Trenton"

Trenton is the capital of New Jersey. Mrs. Morrow gets on the train at Trenton and gets off at Newark, also in New Jersey.

Trenton was founded in 1679 by the Society of Friends (Quakers) and by 1719 had acquired the name of "Trent-towne" from its largest landowner Mr. William Trent. Here, in December of 1776, George Washington achieved the first victory of the American Revolution when he and his continental army crossed the Delaware river – almost certainly seated – and thrashed the cold and sleepy Hessian troops.

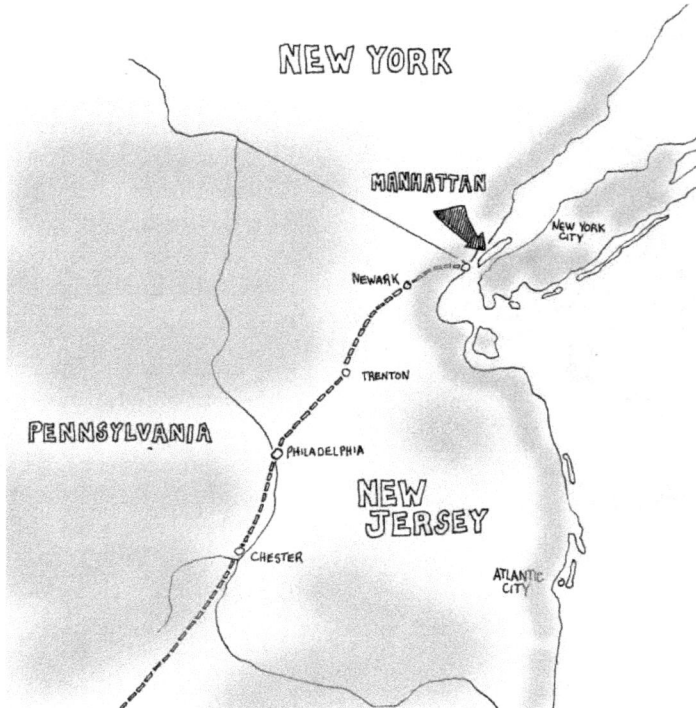

Page 54: "oversexed"

Horny or, as Holden would prefer, *sexy*.

This once-popular term is rarely used nowadays except in cases where your wife/ lover/ girlfriend/ boyfriend/ next-door-neighbor, etc. is more interested in sex than you are.

Page 55: "shooting the old crap"

Pointless talk. See: *shooting the old bull, shooting the breeze, chewing the rag, etc.*

Page 55: "rocks"

Jewels, specifically diamonds.

Page 55: "mixer"

Someone who is socially comfortable and makes friends easily.

Page 55: "I don't believe this is a smoker"

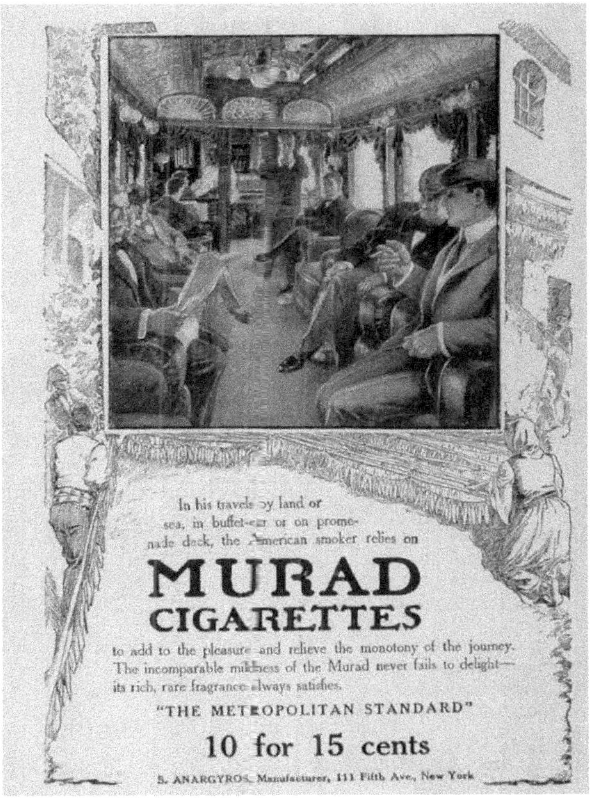

Trains had separate cars for smokers and non-smokers even in the 1940's. This had more to do with the popularity of pipes and cigars than it did with any health concerns and in the 19th century amounted to a kind of de-facto sexual segregation (women smoked, but rarely pipes or cigars). So, even though a large percentage of both sexes smoked in the late 40's and early 50's, custom dictated that you were still expected to go into a "smoking car" to do it.

Holden is suggesting they light up in a car not designated for smoking; a typical faux pas.[35]

Page 56: "wolf"

To suck up smoke with great enthusiasm. (See **"booze hound"** Chapter 4 above.) To eat or drink with great haste and intensity.

Page 57: "shooting it"

You know, *shooting the breeze*. (See **"shooting the old crap"** above)

Page 58: "*Vogue*"

A high-style, fashion magazine that is still published in several countries and languages. According to their web site they are "The world's most important and influential magazine brand. Vogue stands alone as THE fashion Bible."

Vogue Magazine, December 1949

---

[35] "foe-paw" A French term for a social mistake or misjudgment.

Chapter 9

(Sunday, December 18, 1949, just after midnight.)

In which Holden arrives at Penn Station and makes a call to a woman of questionable virtue.

> In faith, I do not love thee with mine eyes
> For they in thee a thousand errors note;
> Nor are mine ears with thy tongue's tune delighted...
> *William Shakespeare, 1595*

Page 59: "Penn Station"

Pennsylvania Station is one of two enormous train terminals in New York City, Grand Central Station being the other. The Pennsylvania Railroad utilized its own station to the south of Manhattan, off 7th Avenue between 33rd and 31st Streets, while the New York Central Railroad ran its trains out of the Grand Central Terminal in the very heart of town. Most trains running in and out of New Jersey stopped or started at Pennsylvania (Penn) Station.

In 1964 all of the aboveground buildings were demolished to make way for the newest incarnation of the Madison Square Garden and a couple of dull office structures. As a result the station as Holden knew it is impossible to see today except in historic photographs and what there is to see is underground.

You really don't know what you've got 'til its gone.

Page 59: "phone booth"

After the invention of the telephone in the late 1870's and before the metastacization of the cellular phone in the 1990's, people who needed to make a call away from home went looking for a phone booth. The phone booth was commonly a wooden or steel structure approximately 30" x 30" x 7' with glass windows and a folding door. Though indoor phone booths were occasionally beautiful pieces of finely crafted and finished furniture, most were spare, utilitarian little cubicles designed for hard use and abuse. Inside the booth were a steel telephone module, sometimes a small table for writing and a narrow seat. There was usually a phone directory from which many of the pages – including the one you needed - had been torn. The telephone accepted coins for payment. For many years the initial charge was a nickel or a dime. If the call was long distance or the duration of the call was more than two or three minutes a telephone operator would interrupt the

call to ask for additional coins.

Phone booths were commonly found in public places with a lot of foot traffic like bus stops, train terminals, airports, sports arenas, department stores, theaters and nightclubs. For many people phone booths acquired a romantic aura simply because the types of calls one made there were not being made at home for very good reasons; gangsters arranged elicit deals, lovers promised rendezvous, detectives and philandering husbands pretended to be someone or somewhere they were not. Superman changed his clothes in one. Tramps and little kids never passed a phone booth without checking the coin return slot for a monetary gift. Walking past a phone booth you would often hear half of an argument, loud demands or the sound of crying (today you can have more or less the same experience just standing in line at a grocery store).

The reality of using a phone booth was quite unromantic. The insides smelled like urine and old sweat, receivers were sticky, the glass windows were scratched or broken, about half the time the phone didn't work and more often than not you lost your dime. The enclosed phone booth became a rarity in the 1970's as the bulky modules were phased out in favor of smaller, unenclosed kiosks. Pay phones died a sad and ugly demise toward the end of the twentieth century. Most were literally vandalized out of existence; others were removed because they had become centers of drug commerce or prostitution. As phones became portable and fewer people were using pay phones it became unprofitable for phone companies to install and maintain booths. If you want to see one now your best bet is film noir from the 1940's and 50's.

Page 59: "a buzz"

A "buzz" is phone call. Also, a *ring*. The *buzz* as a term for a phone call originated in offices where intercoms literally buzzed. *Ring* was the more common term when talking about domestic calls. Eventually the two terms became interchangeable.

Page 59: "Phoebe"

This is the first reference to Phoebe (pronounced, "fee-bee"), Holden's precocious and devoted younger sister. In early permutations of the Holden Caulfield saga she was called Mattie and Holden was Babe Gladwaller. Her name rhymes interestingly with D.B., Holden's writer brother.

The name *Phoebe* comes from Greek and means "luminous, pristine". One of the original Titans, Phoebe was the daughter of Uranus and Gaia. She was associated with the moon. Eventually she became the mother of Leto and Asteria and grandmother of Artemis (who was also called Phoebe) and Apollo.

Also a species of bird.

The insect-eating Eastern Phoebe is one of three species of Phoebe found in North America, Canada and Mexico.

Page 59: "Sally Hayes"

This is the first time we hear of Sally Hayes in *The Catcher in the Rye*. One of Salinger's earlier Holden Caulfield stories, *"A Slight Rebellion off Madison"* (*New Yorker*, December, 1946) featured Sally as Holden's girlfriend/fiance. The nature of their relationship underwent some tweaking between the story and the novel since Sally in *The Catcher in the Rye* is less a long-term, "steady" girlfriend and more of a convenience or familiar expedient. When Holden arrives at Penn Station she is fourth on his list of people he'd like to give a "buzz", behind D.B., Phoebe and Jane Gallagher.

Sally was well known to children of the 40's and 50's as the younger sister of Dick and Jane in the ubiquitous series of readers published by Scott, Foresman and Company from 1930 through 1965. Nearly every kid in America encountered these characters in their journey to literacy. The Curriculum Foundation Series, as it was called, was co-authored by Dr. William S. Gray and William Elson. The hallmark of these books was their highly-structured, limited vocabulary and short sentences, i.e. "Dick will run. See Dick run. Run, Dick, run!" As the children who learned to read from this series aged they found great humor in recalling and parodying the characters, language and insipid storylines of these books.

Page 59: "phony"

Fake; not genuine. This is one of the words most inextricably linked with Holden Caulfield. He first uses "phony" in this chapter and its use increases as his story - and crises - progress toward an inevitable climax in Central Park. The word *phony* means more to Holden than just counterfeit; it seems to encapsulate all he despises and fears about the adult world where compromise and capitulation become the means through which one endures. To Holden *phony* describes both the artifice of adult social interaction and the hypocrisy of expedience.

Page 59: "...breaking a goddam leg..."

When one is in such a hurry that personal injury is a real risk this phrase is appropriate. It usually indicates an inappropriate over-eagerness on the part of the person doing the rushing. This is a facetious remark.

Actors urge each other to "break a leg" for good luck, but Holden means no such thing.

Page 60: "...all the way to Ninedieth Street now."

The cab driver may have left *Pennsylvania Station* and driven up Sixth Avenue (Avenue of the Americas) into *Central Park* and up East Drive to Engineers Gate. He might also have been on 1st or 3rd Avenues. Regardless, there were other opportunities to turn around before 90th Street. Perhaps he thought Holden was a tourist.

Page 60: "little lake"

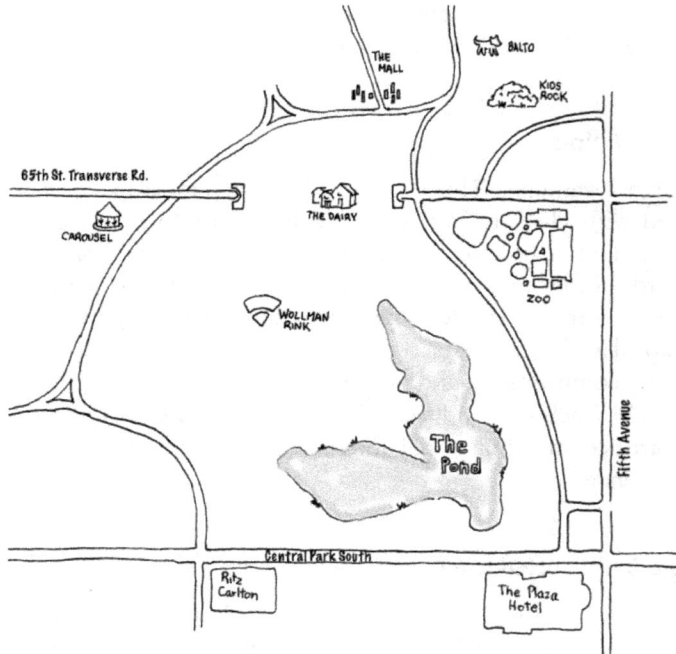

The "little lake" as Holden calls it is officially known as *The Pond*.

Home to plenty of ducks, as well as seagulls and geese, *The Pond* is treasured by locals as a tranquil retreat from the bustling world just yards from its eastern and southern borders. At the northern end of *The Pond* stands the *Gapstow Bridge* (1896), a beautiful stone structure that in summer is cloaked in picturesque green foliage. (See "the lagoon…" Chapter 12)

Page 60: "…the Taft…New Yorker…Edmont…"

The Taft Hotel was at 7th Avenue at 50th Street and the New Yorker was at 481 Eighth Avenue (off 34th Street). *The Edmont* is entirely fictitious and once you've read Holden's impressions of the place you can understand why no existing establishment is eager to take credit for its inspiration.

Page 61: "Real women's clothes…"

Holden is observing a man "cross-dressing". While there are multiple manifestations of this practice in society, what Holden is observing is either a type of fetishism wherein a man experiences sexual excitement through the wearing of women's clothing, especially underclothing, or engaging in a harmless practice which provides him with a sense of well-being and identity that conventional male attire cannot duplicate. Contrary to popular belief, cross-dressing is not an indicator of homosexuality. It is however outside the realm of "conventional behavior" as defined by the era immediately following World War II and a would have been a shock to the naive and uninitiated.

Page 62: "highballs"

Specifically a tall, narrow drinking glass with a capacity of about 8 fluid ounces and used for serving light spirits. The term "highball" is sometimes used to describe the drink contained therein or any cocktail.

Page 62: "...*very* crumby stuff..."

A "crumb" being a tiny morsel of too small to be of any value, "crumby" or "crummy" means "of poor quality" or "unacceptable". What Holden is referring to is sexual behavior he regards as improper. As uncomfortable as he is with his sexuality Holden probably considers some relatively common sexual practices "crummy".

Page 63: "necking"

Prolonged kissing. In Holden's time there were many sexual euphemisms that have faded into disuse with passing time. "Billing and cooing", "wooing", "petting", "fondling", "spooning" and "necking" just aren't heard unless you are hanging out with octogenarians.

Page 63: "B.M."

See note above (**Page 31: ...B.M...**)

Assuming that B.M. is an abbreviation for Bryn Mawr, a college in Pennsylvania, would make Jane older than Holden since he is only sixteen and nowhere near ready for college. More likely Jane is attending Shipley School on the Bryn Mawr campus (see note **Page 31: "Shipley"**).

Page 63: "horny"

Intensely preoccupied with sex; highly aroused. Holden also uses *sexy* to mean much the same thing. The origins of the term are ancient and somewhat in question. Some claim it comes from the manner in which rams and deer butt heads (horns) with each other when competing for mates, others attribute it to the similarities between an animal's horn and the erect penis. I side with the latter since, according to

Pan...horny...horned

the Oxford English Dictionary the phrase "to have the horn" has been synonymous with sexual arousal since at least the mid-18th century.

Page 63: "doing it"

Having sex. ("It" is an amazingly flexible pronoun.)

Page 63: "burlesque"

Burlesque is the term commonly applied to a very popular form of stage entertainment that emphasized broad comedy and sexual innuendo. In many respects it is similar to the British "Panto" or pantomime though burlesque is as American as the banjo or The Book of Mormon. Having its origins in comic satires of opera and dramatic plays, burlesque later came to encompass a wide range of humorous skits, clowning, acrobatics, song and dance. There were always plenty of pratfalls, funny voices, men dressed as women, two-man horse costumes, girls in tights, silly policemen, jugglers and trained dogs.

The burlesque house was above all a place of entertainment for the common people. Ticket prices were kept cheap and literacy - or even an ability to speak English - was not required to fully appreciate the performances. Many acts born on the burlesque stages of New York worked their way onto the Vaudeville circuit and eventually, to television.

It was only in the declining years of burlesque that fan dancers and striptease artists began to appear as part of the evening's - or afternoon's - entertainment. By this time burlesque had come to mean less a PG-rated night out than a good starting place for an evening of debauchery with other traveling salesmen.

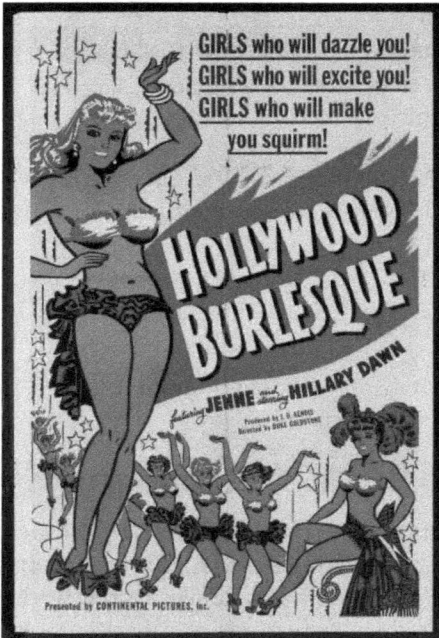

Hiya, sailor,wanna squirm?

In the first two decades of the 20th century vaudeville began to replace burlesque as the popular American entertainment. The really good variety acts went on the vaudeville circuit which was seen as a slightly more wholesome form of entertainment; the fan and balloon dancers stayed with the increasingly raunchy burlesque houses.

Page 64: "Stanford Arms Hotel"

A fictitious hotel; a dump. (Manhattan does have a Pickwick Arms Hotel at 230 East 51st. Street, a Stratford Arms, a Charlton Arms and Ye Old Carlton Arms, but that's not the same thing at all.) [36]

Page 64: "a dump"

A shabby home or room; any place of extreme slovenliness; The Stanford Arms Hotel.

Page 64: "a cocktail"

A mixed drink combining alcoholic beverages with flavorings and/or bottled seltzer, tonic or soda water.

As far as is known, the first appearance of the word cocktail in print was in a New York publication of May,1806. There the cocktail was defined as:

> "a stimulating liquor composed of spirits of any kind, sugar, water, and bitters--it is vulgarly called a bittered sling and is supposed to be an excellent electioneering potion, inasmuch as it renders the heart stout and bold, at the same time that it fuddles the head. It is said, also to be of great use to a Democratic candidate: because a person, having swallowed a glass of it, is ready to swallow anything else."

Cocktails became very popular in the United States during prohibition (1920-1933) when distilled liquors were often of poor quality and taste; bad gin can be greatly improved by the addition of lemon and tonic. Traditionally cocktails were made

---

[36] In case you were wondering, the "Arms" in the name of a hotel or manor house refers not to an appendage or weapons of war but to Heraldic ornament and/or insignia. Sometimes referred to as "crests" or "escutcheons", these devices have been granted to families, countries and corporations since ancient times.

primarily with whiskey, gin or rum. Vodka did not become a popular cocktail base until the 1970's.

Page 64: "a tigress"

An aggressive woman; often a sexually aggressive woman.

Chapter 10

(Sunday morning, December 8, 1949, after midnight)

In which Holden visits the Lavender Room and dances with Bernice, Marty and Laverne.

> Dressed up like a million dollar trooper
> Trying hard to look like Gary Cooper [37]
> Super-duper
> Come, let's mix where Rockefellers
> Walk with sticks or "umberellas"
> In their mitts
> Puttin' on the Ritz
> Irving Berlin, 1930

Page 66: "The Lavender Room"

As might be expected for a non-existent hotel, *The Lavender Room* is a fictional supper club. Manhattan did have its share of color-coded nightspots including *The Blue Angel*, *Le Ruban Bleu*, the *Coral Room* at the Governor Clinton Hotel, the *Rose Room* at the Algonquin and *Cafe Rouge* at the Pennsylvania. The *Hotel Edison* ("1000 Rooms - 1000 Baths - 1000 Showers- 1000 Radios") between 46th and 47th just west of Broadway had a *Green Room* for dining and dancing.

---

[37] See below, **Page 74: "Gary Cooper"**

Lavender is a color often associated with the gay subculture (i.e. Lavender Graduation, Lavender Menace, "going lavender", etc.). Those who wish to see Holden's story as a kind of gay odyssey have used this as one more bit of supporting data, though as described by Holden *The Lavender Room* does not seem to be any more gay than other clubs in New York at the time.

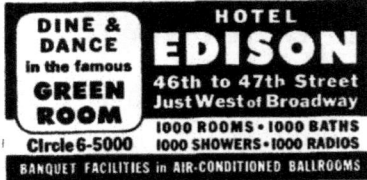

Page 67: "The Baker's Wife"

This 1940 French film took a comic look at marital infidelity. A small town baker refuses to make any more bread after he finds that his wife has run off with a local shepherd. Out of a need for bread more than anything else, the local people band together to try and get the errant wife to return to her husband. This is pretty esoteric stuff for Holden to have seen as a young teen; it almost certainly would have been shown in an "art house" with subtitles, as was the usual case with foreign films.

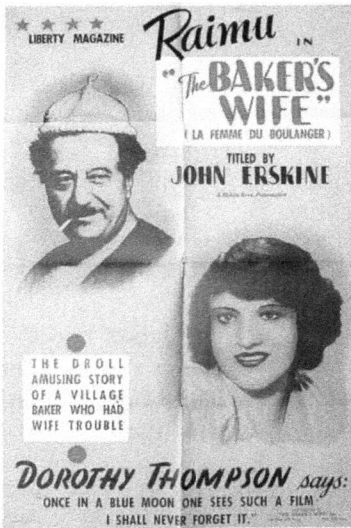

Page 67: "The 39 Steps"

In this early Alfred Hitchcock thriller, a Canadian rancher visiting London is thrust into the unenviable position of being both accused of a murder and very likely the next victim. He and the young blonde who reluctantly teams up with him not only pursue spies who are trying to smuggle government secrets out of the country, but in turn being tracked by those same spies as well as the police.

Page 69: "pimpy-looking"

Resembling a stereotypical pimp of the time; wiry, oily, flashy clothes, gold rings, rheumy-eyed, etc.

Page 69: "...waved a buck..."

It was folk wisdom in those days that a maitre-d' or headwaiter could be bribed to give you a better table or seat you when you had no reservation and the restaurant was full. Most of the time it was true – and still is - though even in 1949 a dollar wouldn't have made that much of an impression.

Page 69: "Buddy Singer"

Great name for a lounge crooner[38], don't you think? The "Buddy" suggests an insinuating familiarity, while the "Singer" tells us what his voice perhaps cannot. Remember "Guy Smiley" from *Sesame Street* or "Nick" the lounge singer as performed by Bill Murray on *Saturday Night Live*?

SPRING IS HERE!
(LONG TIME NO SEE)
.. and so is
Buddy Moreno
Young America's favorite singing STAR
AND HIS GREAT ORCHESTRA
featuring PERRY MITCHELL
Playing for
DINNER & SUPPER DANCING
Nightly except Monday
in the gay new
Century Room
Also open for luncheon daily except Sunday
HOTEL COMMODORE
Right at Grand Central Terminal

Through the spring of 1948 the "gay, new" Century Room at the Hotel Commodore (near the Grand Central terminal) featured Buddy Moreno "and his great orchestra" nightly, except Mondays.

Page 69: "brassy"

Loud and harsh. Pushy.

Page 70: "fond of dancing"

Through the 1930's and 40's it was very common for children of well-to-do families to be trained in the social arts (etiquette) and receive instruction in ballroom-style dancing (fox trot, tango, waltz, gavotte...) from men and women who had been similarly trained centuries earlier. Well-dressed boys and girls would meet after school or on Saturdays to learn what all young men and women were expected to know prior to entering "society" at the age of eighteen. This instruction was based on

---

[38] Vocalist

a European model of socialization that stipulated a rather rigid code of behavior, formalized language and shared regard for ritual. At regular intervals students would be expected to show their mastery of these formalities at an event known as *cotillion*. Holden, as a child of parents whose means were well above average, would have attended these classes in his younger years. His formal dancing experience is attested to by his comments in this chapter.

Page 70: "grools"

This is an intentionally childish (or faux drunken) mispronunciation of the word *"girls"*.

Page 71: "Marco and Miranda"

A fictional dance team. As an entertainment, dance teams had been popular since at least the late 1800's. Every era had its favorite couple of ballroom-style dancers; Vernon and Irene Castle (1910's and 20's), Fred and Adele Astaire (1920's and 30's), Shirley Temple and Bill Robinson (1930's), Fred Astaire and Ginger Rogers (1930's and 1940's) and Marge and Gower Champion (1950's), and Bobby Burgess and Barbara Boylan / Cissy King (1960's and 70's). From time to time ballroom dancing seemed poised to make a comeback as a major entertainment for both the participant and observer but nothing much materialized until the television program "Dancing with the Stars" became a worldwide phenomenon. The U.S. version, based on the popular British program *Strictly Come Dancing,* premiered in the summer of 2005.

In film, Baz Luhrman's *Strictly Ballroom* (1992), *Shall We Dance?* (1996 - Japanese and 2004 - American), and *Mad Hot Ballroom* (2005) are contemporary examples of how the art form has endured.

Page 71: "Just One of Those Things"

One of Cole Porter's enduring classic songs. It has been recorded by just about everybody who ever sang a ballad; Billie Holiday, Frank Sinatra, Willie Nelson, Rosemary Clooney, Judy Garland, etc. The song goes like this:

> *As Dorothy Parker* **39* *once said to her boyfriend:*
> *"Fare thee well!"*
> *As Columbus announced when he knew he was*
> *bounced: "It was swell, Isabelle, swell!*
> *"As Abelard said to Heloise: "Don't forget to drop*
> *a line to me, please."*
> *As Juliet cried in her Romeo's ear: "Romeo, why*
> *not face the fact, my dear?"*
> *It was just one of those things,*
> *just one of those crazy flings,*
> *one of those bells that now and then rings,*
> *just one of those things.*
> *It was just one of those nights,*
> *just one of those fabulous flights,*
> *a trip to moon on gossamer wings, just one of those*
> *things.*
> *If we'd thought a bit of the end of it when we started*
> *painting the town,*
> *We'd have been aware that our love affair was too*
> *hot not to cool down.*
> *So, goodbye, dear, and amen! Here's hoping we meet*
> *now and then.*
> *It was great fun, but it was just one of those things!*

Page 71: "Peter Lorre"

A character actor of the 30's, 40's and 50's with moist, bulging eyes and a very distinctive, breathy voice. Born László Löwenstein and raised in Austria-Hungary he worked in

---

[39] Dorothy Parker was a poet / writer / humorist of the 1920's and 30's known for her cynicism and biting wit.

German films until the rise of Nazism in 1933. His creepy appearance and unctuous vocal delivery made him a natural villain or henchman. While he could easily have fallen in with hundreds of other character actors whose names are now forgotten, he was fortunate enough have made several great, now classic, films by the time he reached his forties. Noteworthy Lorre films include *M* (German, 1931), *The Man Who Knew Too Much* (English, 1933), *The Maltese Falcon* (1941), *Casablanca* (1943), *Arsenic and Old Lace* (1944) and *20,000 Leagues Under the Sea* (1954). Because his peculiar voice was easily imitated vocal impressions of him became common in animated cartoons from Warner Brothers in the 1940's and continue right up to the present day.

Page 72: "jitterbugging"

Dance fads come and go. Jitterbugging was a very creative, long-lived and vigorous dance style that began in Black jazz clubs in the 1930's and spread to the rest of America shortly thereafter. Cab Calloway is believed to be the first bandleader to use the term *jitterbug* with his band, but Benny Goodman is officially credited with launching the jitterbug craze during a tour of California ballrooms in 1934.

Over the next 20 years the dance that had been called "Jitterbug" evolved into what is now generically known as "Swing". *The Lindy Hop, the Push, Jive , the Shag , the New Yorker* and the *Bop* were all variations on jitterbugging. The dance thrived during the era of big bands (1930's through the early 1950's) when "swing was king".

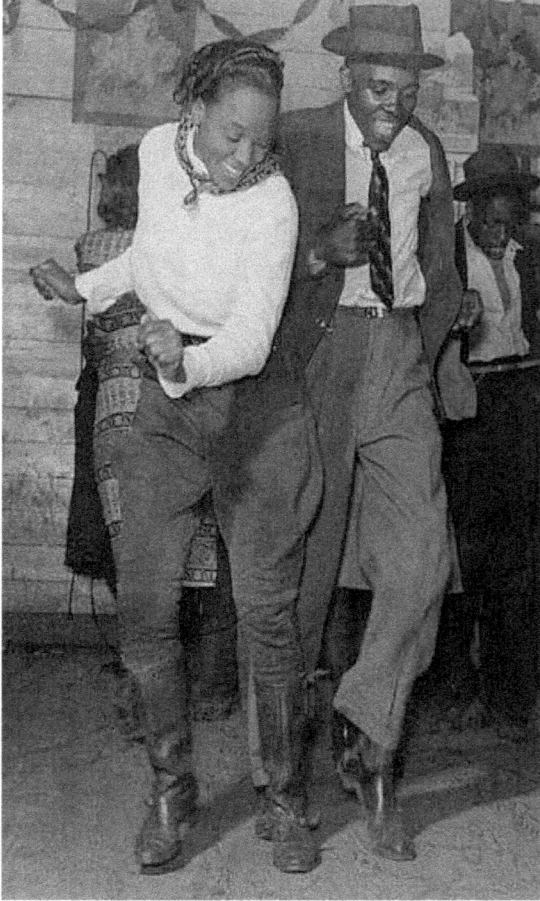

Page 73: "Crabs or Krebs"

This chick and cat are "blowin' their wigs". Dig?

This is a joke. *Crabs* is a slang term for crab lice, a creepy vermin that infests the dark, moist areas of the body (read: groin, armpit, etc.) and are transmitted through contact with others who are "unclean" (read: bums, whores, etc.). Also ironic in the light of Holden's fondness for the term *lousy*.

Page 73: "Jim Steele"

Holden has chosen as his alias for the evening a name which would be right at home in one of those "dumb stories" Holden mocked in Chapter 8. (See **"dumb Stories in a magazine"**, Chapter 8)

Page 73: "Stork Club or El Morocco"

Dubbed "the most famous night spot in the world", The Stork Club was located at 3 East 53rd Street in New York City. According to columnist Robert Dana (in 1948), the Stork club was "a place where Hollywoodites, politicians, and other celebrities could sit quietly and chat, drink, or play gin rummy." The El Morocco, on east 54th Street, was another place for celebrities to hang out with each other and the usual wannabes.

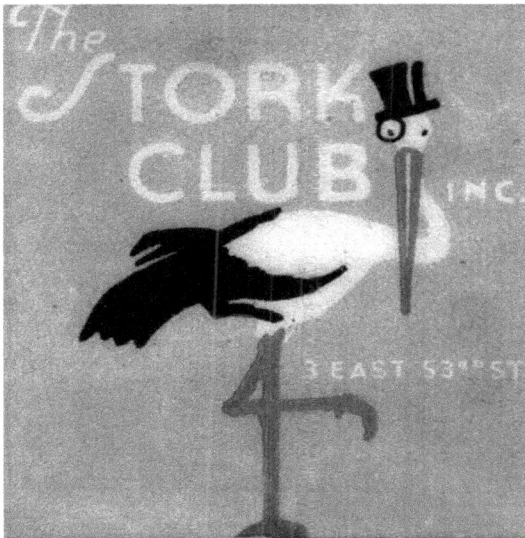

In those days people dressed up for a night out. The look was shiny and classy. Neither club still exists.

Page 74: "Gary Cooper"

American movie star (1901 – 1961) Gary Cooper was a reliable leading man whose career spanned a remarkable 35 years from the mid 1920's to the end of the 1950's. Characterized as the rugged, laconic individual he preceded John Wayne as a symbol of American masculinity. He was voted the Academy Award Best Actor *Oscar* twice, in 1941 for *Sergeant York* and again in 1952 for *High Noon*, generally considered his finest performance. Among his other best films are: *A Farewell to Arms* (1932), *Mr. Deeds Goes to Town* (1936), *The Pride of the Yankees* (1942), *Saratoga Trunk* (1945), and *Friendly Persuasion* (1956),

Page 74: "sterling sense of humor"

A *sterling* sense of humor is of the highest grade. Holden is being sarcastic. *Sterling* is the name given to a particularly high grade of silver, 92.5% pure, used for ornament, tableware and decorative objects. Since the 13th century the word *sterling* has been stamped on silver objects to denote their high silver content. Anything *sterling* is of unimpeachable quality.

Page 74: "Tom Collinses - in...December..."

The *Tom Collins* cocktail was originally called the *John Collins*. Essentially a lemonade with sparkle, you mix two parts soda water with one part gin and one part lemon juice. Add sugar and crushed ice.

A Tom Collins is a cocktail traditionally enjoyed during the warm weather months of July, August and September. Like a white suit or a panama hat, a Tom Collins is a social faux pas[40] after Labor Day, so don't say you haven't been warned.

---

[40] French for "Oops, my bad", remember?

Page 75: "licorice stick"

African-American jazz slang for clarinet. "Old Marty" did not coin the term, but it had obviously become passé (worn out from overuse) by the time she used it. (Or perhaps its just one of those terms white people cannot utter convincingly.)

Page 75: "Radio City Music Hall"

The glitzy, *Art Deco**[41] theater central to Rockefeller Plaza was opened in 1932. Since 1933 they have offered a spectacular Christmas show each year. The massive stage and its substructure were state-of-the-art at the time of its construction. The name *Radio City Music Hall* came from *The Radio Corporation of America*, one of the first major tenants in the Rockefeller Center business complex. A visit to this grand theatre has long been considered a "must" for any out-of-town tourist. An essential component of any Radio City Music Hall show was an appearance by the *Rockettes*, a women's precision dance team which for more than 50 years performed four shows a day, 365 days a year.

Page 75: "check came to about thirteen bucks"

This would be the equivalent of about 60 dollars today. Holden got punked.

---

[41] *Art Deco* is a distinctive architectural style popular in the 1930's.

Chapter 11

(Sunday morning; the wee hours)

In which Holden thinks fondly of Jane.

> If I loved you...
> Time and again I would try to say
> All I'd want you to know...
> Words wouldn't come in an easy way
> Round in circles I'd go!
> Oscar Hammerstein II, 1945

Page 76: "I know old Jane like a book."

To know someone "like a book" is to know him or her very well; thoroughly. Sometimes you'll hear someone say "I know _____ like the palm of my hand" which means the same thing.

Page 76: "...relieve himself..."

A polite way to refer to urination or defecation.

Page 76: "big stink"

To make a lot of trouble or fuss; to cause an uproar.

Page 77: "big freeze"

When you publicly encounter someone you don't like and you ignore him or her this is called *cutting* or giving them the *cold shoulder.* The *big freeze* Holden is referring to is the same as the *cold shoulder.*

Page 77: "what I go around in…"

That is, my score for nine or eighteen holes of golf; number of strokes per game.

Page 77: "movie short"

Back in the days when your great-grandpa was buying gas for 15 cents a gallon, an afternoon at the movies was really an afternoon at the movies. Not only was there a double-feature (two different movies for the price of one), but you could also count on a couple of cartoons, a newsreel (see page 112, below) and one or two *short subjects.*[42]

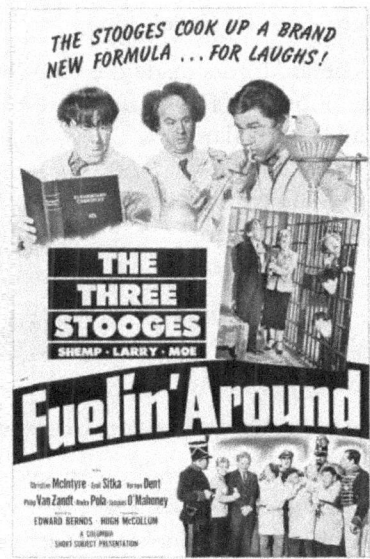

THE STOOGES COOK UP A BRAND NEW FORMULA … FOR LAUGHS!

THE THREE STOOGES
SHEMP · LARRY · MOE

Fuelin' Around

Christine McIntyre and Sitka Vernon Dent
Philip Van Zandt Emil Polo Jock O'Mahoney
EDWARD BERNDS · HUGH McCOLLUM
A COLUMBIA
SHORT SUBJECT PRESENTATION

Short subjects were generally ten or twelve-minute films of a humorous nature built around real-life people and places. Occasionally they were educational or political, but more often they were just silly. Now when you go to the movies all you get for your 12 bucks is twenty minutes of tedious trailers and a sequel.

---

[42] And then, if you were a real cinephile (or just someone looking for a place to sleep) you could stay in your seat and watch the whole show over again.

Page 77: "And she never really closed it all the way, her mouth."

This is an odd thing for Holden to say about someone he really cares for, though it does provide Jane with an endearing flaw. From a clinical perspective this symptom suggests a blockage in the nasal sinuses that is often aggravated by enlarged adenoids or inflamed tonsils. Those suffering from allergic rhinitis (hay fever) often have clogged nasal passages forcing them to breath through their mouths. Mouth breathing is also viewed as one indicator of sleep apnea, a potentially serious sleep disorder in which the air passages are blocked during sleep and breathing comes in irregular gasps.

Page 78: "La Salle"

General Motors made the *La Salle* from 1927 to 1940. It was the poor man's Cadillac. Today one in good condition would be considered a collector's item.

Page 78: "kid the pants off a girl"

This has nothing to do with sex, or pants for that matter. To *kid the pants off* of someone is to tease or kid someone relentlessly. No one's pants actually come off...usually.

Page 79: "icicle"

Saying that someone is an *icicle* is just another way of denouncing him or her as lacking emotional warmth or humanness.

When used to describe a woman it suggests that she is incapable of sexual arousal. In the 1970's feminists told us that the term was obsolete and employed primarily by men as a disparaging label for women who were not receptive to their sexual overtures.

The term has never been applied to men for obvious reasons.

The term 'frigid" is not nearly as commonly heard as it once was, though it is difficult to determine whether that is due to enlightenment or changing fashion.

Page 79: "newsreel"

A day at the movies was not complete without a newsreel. Before the popularization of television these compilations of current events were most people's only chance to see the personalities, places and events that made the news.

Page 80: "get to first base"

Back when the lives of men and women were more rigidly separated than they are now and the light in one's home came from candles or gas, men devised an elaborate system of communication with each other based on code-speak. One of the more popular metaphors seems to have been baseball and levels of sexual conquest were spoken of as plays. To kiss a girl was to get to *first base*. *Second base* was achieved by placing the hand on the still clothed breasts (bosom) of the girl. Third base was a similar kind of fondling, but under her clothing. I don't need to spell out a *home run* for you. (If you got to home plate you were, depending on the decade, *hookin' up, knocking boots, rocking the Kasbah, gettin' jiggy wid it, doin' the wild thang,* or *making whoopee.*) These definitions were highly flexible and subjective; about all you could get everyone to agree on were *first base* and *home run*.

Girls also had coded ways of speaking about sexual matters among themselves, but you can bet it was more subtle and not dependent on sports metaphors.

Page 80: "whory-looking blondes"

Cheap and flashy. I'd get into more detail but I don't want to run the risk of disrespecting someone's mother.

Page 80: "Greenwich Village"

A wonderful old section of south Manhattan has been known as *Greenwich Village* or just *The Village*, for most of the 20th century. Prior to that it was called *Washington Square*. The neighborhood has been in existence for three hundred years. *Greenwich* (pronounced "gren-itch") *Village* is bordered on the east by Broadway and on the west by the Hudson River. Its northern and southern boundaries are 14th Street and Houston ("How'-stun") Street. The Village has long maintained a bohemian atmosphere and was at the center of at least three of the twentieth century's more significant social movements. In the 1950's the *Beat Generation* found a home in its coffee houses and clubs. Writers and poets such as Allen Ginsberg, Gregory Corso and Jack Kerouac were very much at home there. In the 1950's and 60's those same venues saw the birth of the *folk music scene* ushered in by Pete Seeger, Joan Baez, and Mimi and Dick Farina. More recently the *Gay Pride* and *Gay Liberation* movements have created landmarks at *Christopher Street* and the *Stonewall Inn*, considered by many to be the birthplace of modern gay awareness.

Since the 20's the Village has provided a home for jazz musicians. *Birdland* and *The Fire Spot* were early clubs. *The Bitter End*, *Blue Note* and *The Village Vanguard*, a jazz club founded in 1935, came later.

Page 80: "Ernie's a big, fat colored guy that plays the piano"

There has never been a shortage of jazz pianists who meet the description Holden provides of Ernie. Though *Ernie* is a fictional character, his real-life inspirations could have been *Art Tatum, Oscar Peterson* or *Errol Garner*, among others (though Mr. Garner was never really someone you would describe as "big, fat"). On December 17, 1949 Errol Garner was playing at the Three Deuces, 72 W. 52nd Street.

It should be mentioned that the term "colored" when applied to an African-American was not derogatory in the 1940's, 50's and early 60's. In fact, it was the term preferred by a majority of polite, enlightened people both Black and otherwise. It, along with the term "negro", fell into disfavor among Black Power proponents in the late 1960's.

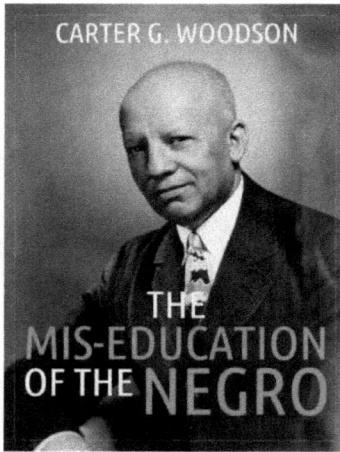

Chapter 12

(Very early Sunday morning)

In which Holden visits Ernie's and meets Lillian Simmons.

> Sing the Whiffenpoofs assembled with their glasses raised on high
> And the magic of their singing casts its spell...
> We're poor little lambs who have lost our way
> Baa, baa, baa
> We're little black sheep who have gone astray
> Baa, baa, baa
> Meade Minnigerode (Yale 1910)

Page 81: "tossed his cookies"

It smelled like someone had recently vomited. Americans seem to have as many euphemisms for *vomit* as Eskimos are alleged to have words for snow. (Does this perhaps suggest that our real national pastime isn't baseball after all?) A few of the more popular ones are: *barf, upchuck, spit up, throwup, ralph, heave, spew, hurl, blow chunks, retch,* and *lose lunch.*

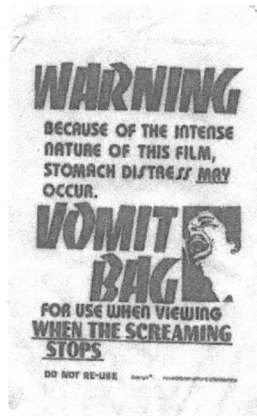

Page 81: "…it was Saturday night"

It wasn't Saturday night, of course. It was probably closer to 3:00 AM Sunday morning. One can hardly blame Holden for losing track of the time.

Page 81: "…the lagoon…(d)own by Central Park South?"

Holden is referring to what is known as *The Pond*. The Pond is located in the far southeastern corner of Central Park across from the Plaza Hotel. Interestingly, there is a statue of Robert Burns, author of *Comin' Thro' the Rye,* just north of *The Pond* on the *Author's Walk*. (See **"little lake"**, Chapter 9)

The Gapstow Bridge over The Pond in winter.

Page 83: "…their bodies take in nutrition…right through the goddam seaweed…"

Neither Holden nor his cab driver seems to know much about fish in wintertime. The short version is this: When the surface of the pond freezes over and the temperature of the surrounding water drops close to 32 degrees the fish go into a state of semi-hibernation during which they require much less oxygen than usual and hardly anything in the way of food. The pond never fully freezes at least in part because of the gasses given off by decaying vegetable matter on the bottom and the unique property of water to freeze from the outside toward the center. There is always liquid water down there somewhere, which explains why careless skaters get wet when they fall through.

Page 83: "...a bat out of hell..."

This is a colorful an ofter-heard American colloquialism

meaning "to escape rapidly and with great urgency".

Page 83: "…check your coat..."

In the late 1940's, especially in part of the world where it got cold, people wore what were called "overcoats". These heavy wool or fur garments were generally too bulky to wear indoors, so nightclubs, restaurants and hotels had small rooms off to the side of their entrance where hats and coats could be "checked" with an attendant. You would give them your hat, coat or umbrella in exchange for a ticket or a token with a number on it. At the end of the evening you could trade the token for your stuff.   This sort of procedure isn't seen much any more, although I am told there are clubs in Los Angeles where a similar service is provided for those carrying automatic weapons.

Page 85: "dope fiend"

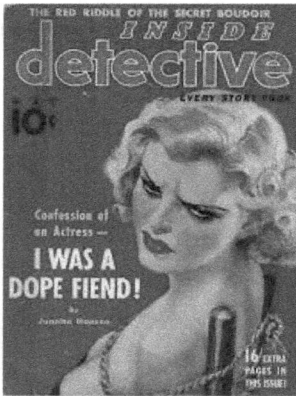

A colorful alternate for *drug addict*. Dope has been used as a synonym for opium and/or cocaine since the 1880's. The term has since become shorthand for any sort of illicit drug.

Page 85: "drink up the minimum"

Nightclubs, cabarets and other entertainment venues where food and beverages are served commonly have two ways of making money. One is to charge a "cover", which means you have to pay just to sit down at a table. The other is to stipulate the minimum number of drinks each person must order during the evening, performance or set. (Alcoholic drinks are a high profit item; the house can easily make a 90% profit or higher on every mixed drink sold.) If there is a two drink minimum per table, per set, and you don't have a lot of money to spend you will want to consume those drinks very slowly so that the waiter will not immediately bring you another when your glass is empty. The process of consuming a beverage slowly is called "nursing" a drink.

Page 85: "Joe-Yale-looking guy"

Clean-cut, athletic, conservatively dressed. (See **"Ivy League"** below.)

The name Joe is often used to indicate a type or standard as in *a regular Joe, surfer Joe, Joe Schmoe* [43] or *Joe college.* (see **"Holy Joe voices..."**; Chapter 14)

Page 85: "flitty-looking"

Whe word "flit" means to move around quickly and lightly; gambol, caper, cavort, prance, etc. In the 20th century it also became, briefly, a derisive term for a homosexual male. "Flitty-looking" is used to describe any man whose dress or mannerisms suggest that he is gay. It is neither polite nor currently in wide use. (See pages 206-207 **"Full of Flits"**)

Page 85: "...Tattersall vests."

Tattersall is a checked pattern of colored lines crisscrossing to make perfect squares. The squares can be very small or quite large. A tattersall vest is required riding equipment for those who hunt foxes or wish to appear that they do.

In 1948 Truman Capote's first novel, *Other Voices Other Rooms* was published to widespread acclaim. Causing something of a sensation was the photograph on the back of the dust jacket which showed the 28 year-old author - looking a lot closer to fourteen - reclining seductively on a chaise longue in a *tattersall vest*.[44] The outlandish coquettery of the pose made it clear from the start that this was not a personality likely to have had much use for, or familiarity with, a closet. As another young writer Salinger could not help but have read the novel and seen the

---

[43] **Joe Schmoe, Shmoe,* or *Schmo* is a nobody; an inconsequential person. In Yiddish a "shmoe" is a bumpkin; an easily tricked yokel.
[44] And looking...well, flitty.

photograph. Perhaps he remembered the vest and chose to employ it as sartorial shorthand for gayness.

Page 85: "Ivy League"

Officially, there are eight schools in the *Ivy League*. These are old, stately colleges and universities where history, illustrious alumni and a certain amount of elitism combine to create an aura of wealth and class. The *Ivy* comes from the tenacious vine that grows over the bricks[45] of which their oldest buildings are constructed. *League* is another word for an association or organization. *Brown, Columbia, Cornell, Harvard, the University of Pennsylvania, Princeton* and *Yale* are *Ivy League* schools. All of these schools are to be found in the northeast part of the United States and all, except Cornell, were founded during the colonial era. The term *Ivy League* has come to denote not only the colleges themselves, but also the students, their manner of dress, their habits, attitudes and behaviors.

Page 86: "giving her a feel"

Touching a girl or woman on any part of her body ordinarily covered by underwear is what is meant by the phrase "giving her a feel". If the girl is agreeable it is called *fondling* or *foreplay*, if she is not it is called sexual assault.

---

[45] Bricks laid by, in many cases, slaves.

Page 86: "knockers"

You know, breasts. Also known as *tits, boobs, hooters, cupcakes, mammaries, dugs, teats, balloons, melons, headlights, boulders, a rack, a pair, the twins, the girls,* etc.

Page 86: "a poker up his ass"

Rigid, way too serious; perpetually disgruntled.

A *poker* is a fireplace tool. It is a steel or iron rod about 30 inches in length with a hooked prod at one end. Pokers range from strictly utilitarian to highly ornate. Someone who is lacking a sense of humor is described as walking around with "a poker up his ass" and one can easily imagine that such a modification to one's bowels would result in an immediate loss of *bonhomie*.

Page 87: "pansy"

A *pansy* is a *flit*. Largely archaic, it is also not generally regarded as a socially acceptable term except, occasionally, among gay people themselves.

Chapter 13

(Sunday morning before sunrise)

In which Holden is visited by Sunny and tells her about his clavichord problem.

> I could tell you a lot, but it's not
> In a gentleman's code...
> And if I'm gloomy, please listen to me
> Till it's talked away
> > One for My Baby
> > (and one more for the road).
> > Harold Arlen, 1943

Page 88:"Forty-one gorgeous blocks"

If in fact Holden is being truthful and he did walk forty-one blocks north from Greenwich Village that would have taken him very close to Times Square and Rockefeller Plaza. In all likelihood Holden's "pervert"-occupied hotel was located south of Central Park between 8th and Park Avenue.

Page 88: "...one of those very yellow guys"

For hundreds of years the color yellow has been associated with cowardice. Someone who behaves in a cowardly way is said to have, or be, a "yellow-belly". The origin is uncertain, but it is quite clear the when the crewmen aboard the S.S. Caine call their mentally unbalanced Captain Queeg "old yellow-stain" (Herman's Wouk's *The Caine Mutiny*, 1951) they are referring to the urine which is often involuntarily voided in a moment of sheer terror.

Page 88: "galoshes"

Rain boots. (See **"galoshes"**, Chapter 5, page 58)

Page 89: "cutting and snotty"

Rude. A *cutting* remark is one designed to make the recipient feel small. *Snotty* denotes an immature approach to insult; impertinence.

Page 89: "If you're supposed to sock somebody in the jaw...you should do it."

It is worth noting that Holden's monologue in this chapter covers some of the same ground Hamlet explored in his "O, what a rogue and peasant slave am I" (*Hamlet* 2.2.555-612) speech.

> *I, a dull and muddy-mettled rascal, peak,*
> *Like John-a-dreams, unpregnant of my cause,*
> *And can say nothing; ... Am I a coward?*
> *Who calls me villain? ...*
> *... I should take it: for it cannot be*
> *But I am pigeon-liver'd...*

(Hey, HOLDEN and HAMLET both begin with an "H" and have six letters! And both have recently left school! I see a potential Master's thesis here.)

Page 90: "stinking"

Drunk. Americans have almost as many substitute words and expressions for *inebriation* as they do for *vomit*; Swacked, pie-eyed, three sheets to the wind, snockered, blasted, feeling no pain, wasted, polluted, ripped, etc. God bless us, every one!

Page 90: "elevator guy"

Up until the 1960's an elevator without an attendant would have been nearly unthinkable. Someone had to stand there to open the door and ask, "What floor, please?". The attendant would then announce each floor as it was reached, often explaining what business or services could be found there. Like hotel doormen, elevator attendants had distinctive uniforms that often included a silly little cylindrical *pillbox* hat.

Page 91: "tail"

A common American expression meaning *sexual intercourse* was "getting a piece of tail" or a "piece of ass". While still in use, the phrase is far less common than it was twenty or thirty years ago. Today it's all about "booty".

Page 91: "a throw"

One sex act. As differentiated from "a night" which might include several sex acts, or a "session" which includes a psychiatrist and a couch.

You'll want to come back to this passage later in order to determine who is telling the truth about the going rates for illicit venery.

Page 93: "beat women off with a club"

A man with more women than he can possibly handle must "beat them off with a club" caveman style. The expression was, "he's so popular (sexy, attractive, etc.) he has to beat women off with a club". The practice is very much frowned upon today. The beating part, that is.

Page 93: "rake"

A really old-fashioned term of disapproval. As far back as 17th century England, a "rake" was a man who lacked any sense of moral propriety. He used drugs, drank too much, consorted

with William Hogarth, illustration from *The Rake's Progress*, both male and female. And I don't mean that in a good way. The current equivalents "playboy" or "player" lack the level of disapproval that "rake" carried.

Page 93: "Caulfield and his Magic Violin..."

Holden is making another layered joke here. Most 1951 readers of *The Catcher in the Rye* would have been familiar with "Evelyn and her Magic Violin" whose radio appearances were a regular feature of *The Hour of Charm* (1934 – 48). Evelyn Kaye Klein, a talented classical musician and student at the Juilliard School of Music, was hired by – and eventually married to - the now-legendary Phil Spitalny whose All-Girl Orchestra provided some of the most charming minutes in *The Hour of Charm*.

Page 93: "Polo coat"

Another camel's hair coat, tailored with stitched edges and a half-belt in the back.

Page 95: "Sunny"

You might find it interesting to know that while J.D. Salinger was attending Valley Forge Military Academy his nickname among other students was "Sonny".

Page 95: "Brand clean"

The term "brand-new" has meant, since at least the 16th century, perfectly new, as in hot-iron-fresh from the forge or furnace. "Brand-fire-new", "brand-span-new", "brand-spander-new" and the more recent "brand-spanking-new" are variants. Sunny is corrupting this terminology by changing the new to clean as if to mean freshly clean or as clean as if it were new.

Page 96: "wuddayacallit"

What-do-you-call-it, used as a noun. Spelling varies greatly and variants include *wutchamacallit* (see **Chapter 14**, below). Very much like a *thingamabob* or a *doohickey*. "Wuddayacallit" or "Whuchamacallit" is a word one uses in place of a noun one can't remember or an object one does not know the proper name for. For example: "Hey, Mac. Hows about handin' me that watchamacallit over there?"

Page 96: "clavichord"

One of the few obvious gags in what may be Catcher's funniest chapter. A *clavichord* is a European keyboard instrument, small and soft in tone. It was made in Germany from about 1750 to the 1840's.

Holden, however, is clearly referring to a part of his body. He is confusing *clavichord* with *clavicle*, a bone that runs on either side of the upper torso connecting the shoulder to the top of the rib cage.

The dialogue between Sunny and Holden is an obvious parody of a similar conversation between Jake Barnes and Georgette, a prostitute, in the opening chapter of *The Sun Also Rises* by

Ernest Hemingway. In that novel the protagonist, Jake, has lost his testicles due to a war injury and rather than come right out and say so, hints at his disability in elliptical euphemisms.

Page 97: "Mel-vine Douglas"

Melvin Douglas[46] was a Hollywood leading man whose career in film spanned an amazing 50 years. The film Sunny is referring to where Melvin Douglas' kid brother falls off a boat must be the result of confusion. Melvin Douglas made no films during W.W. II (1943 - 45) and none that fit that description between 1946 and 50. Sunny could be referring to Robert Young who played Melvin Douglas' brother in 1938 in *The Shining Hour* but it is unlikely that she would remember so vividly a supporting character in a film she'd seen when she was ten years old or younger.

Page 98: "frock"

A dress. This is a rather old-fashioned term for Sunny to be using. That her speech is rendered through endearingly anachronistic terms helps to take the edge off of her mendacity.

Page 98: "crumb-bum"

A worthless person. *Crumb* is slang for *worthless* or *no good*; *bum* is an all-purpose term of derision.

---

[46] Douglas married well. His wife, Helen Gahagan Douglas, in many respects left a more lasting legacy than her husband. After she lost a bitterly contested election for the office of U.S. Senator from California to Richard M. Nixon – whose 1950 campaign was has since been dissected as an exemplum of "smear" – she gave him the nickname "Tricky Dick" that stuck with him the rest of his unfortunately long political career.

"I prefer to be called a 'neglected morsel'".

Chapter 14

(Sunday morning, before sunrise)

In which Holden reminisces about Allie and the twelve disciples, ponders his cowardice and is roughed up by Maurice.

Oh, yellow man, oh, yellow man
We understand, you know we understand…
Got to have a yellow woman
When you're a yellow man
Yellow Man by Randy Newman, 1970

Give me police protection
Gonna buy a gun so
I can look after number one.
Give me a bodyguard
A black belt Judo expert with a machine gun
My Wife by John Entwistle, 1971

Page 98: "Lake Sedebego"

A fake lake. Don't jump on your bike and go looking for it. There is, however, a Lake Sebago in Maine.

Page 98: "BB guns"

The forties equivalent of a skateboard or an MP3 player; every boy wanted a BB gun. They were heavily advertised on the back pages of comic books. These weapons were designed for target shooting, but marketed as toys. In terms of firepower a BB gun was pretty mild; you could kill a bird if you could hit it, but the worst damage you could do to a squirrel would be a painful wound and emotional trauma. Every mother's fear was that her son would shoot his own, or someone else's, eye out. This mother/son conflict is vividly depicted in the Bob Clark 1983 film of Jean Shepherd's *The Christmas Story,* which incidentally takes place in the 1940's.

If advertising expenditure count for anything, Daisy

Your Boy—What Kind of a Man Will He Make?

DAISY AIR RIFLES

Your Boy should learn to shoot with the SAFER DAISY AIR RIFLE

was the uncontested king of air rifles in the 1940's and 50's. Such magazines as *Popular Mechanics, Field and Stream,* and *Boy's Life,* as well as countless comic books featured ads extolling the virtues of manliness and self-reliance as they could be learned through proper "training in the clean, manly sport" of target shooting.

Page 99: "...that lunatic...that lived in the tombs and kept cutting himself with stones."

It is no surprise that Holden would be drawn to this story, or that he would identify the man with "an unclean spirit" as a "lunatic". Like himself, this "guy (he) likes best" in the Bible, after Jesus, is an innocent victim tortured from within and misunderstood by those around him.

Holden here demonstrates more than a passing familiarity with Biblical text. The episode he refers to appears three times in the New Testament (Matthew 8:28; Luke 8:26 and Mark 5:1). There are small variations in the different retellings; Matthew refers to two "demon-possessed men" when Mark and Luke tell of just one man; all refer to the herd of swine but only Mark numbers them at "about 2000". Mark's oft-quoted version is the only one to mention both "tombs" and "bruising with stones":

> *And when he was come out of the ship, immediately there met him out of the tombs a man with an unclean spirit,*
>
> *Who had his dwelling among the tombs; and no man could bind him, no, not with chains... ...neither could any man tame him.*
>
> *And always, night and day, he was in the mountains, and in the tombs, crying, and cutting himself with stones.*
>
> *But when he saw Jesus afar off, he ran and worshipped him,*
>
> *And cried with a loud voice, and said, What have I to do with thee, Jesus...? I adjure thee by God, that thou torment me not.*
>
> *For he said unto him, Come out of the man, thou unclean spirit. And he asked him, What is thy*

name? And he answered, saying, My name is
Legion: for we are many.

And all the devils besought him, saying, Send us
into the swine, that we may enter into them.

And forthwith Jesus gave them leave. And the
unclean spirits went out, and entered into the swine:
and the herd ran violently down a steep place into
the sea, (they were about two thousand) and were
choked in the sea.

A chillingly dramatic story with weird, supernatural touches (talking swine?) Mark's version with the unearthly, "My name is Legion; for we are many" has inspired modern tales of demonic possession, notably William Peter Blatty's 1971 thriller, *The Exorcist.* Here the emphasis is on Jesus' channeling the power of God to transfer the man's demons to a herd of swine that are then drowned

Page 99: "Quaker"

The Religious Society of Friends, commonly known as the *"Quakers",* was founded in England by George Fox in the early 1650's. The designation *"Quaker",* somewhat disrespectful in origin, comes from the allegation that members were urged to "tremble at the word of God". Early practitioners settled in what is now the state of Pennsylvania.

Though there have been many divisions within *The Society of Friends,* in the past 200 years, there are certain beliefs which tend to be common among followers of this faith. First, *Quakers* hold the word of Jesus above the Bible itself and therefore greatly value His voice as he speaks to each individual. For this reason sustained periods of silence are common at meetings. Plainness of dress, modesty and humility are stressed. *Quakers* have always been great believers in equality and this led them to take a position of moral leadership in the American antislavery movement. *Quaker's* are pacifists. In 1947 the Nobel Peace Prize was awarded to the American Friends Service Committee.

George Fox

The most common pictorial representation of a *Quaker* is the benign, smiling fellow on the cylindrical box of oats in the supermarket.

Famous *Quakers* include Thomas Paine, James Dean, Richard M. Nixon, Susan B. Anthony, Walt Whitman, and William Penn.

Best *"Quaker"* movie: *Friendly Persuasion*, 1956.

Page 100: "Holy Joe voices"

For some unaccountable reason many ministers - and I believe Southern Baptist ministers are among the most flagrant offenders - adopt a resonant, nasal, slightly "fruity" tone when addressing their assembled brethren. It is the artificiality of this voice that Holden refers to when he talks about the "Holy Joe voices ". Reverend Lovejoy of *The Simpsons* (voiced by Harry Shearer) provides a wonderful example of a "Holy Joe" voice.

Page 101: "chief"

"Chief" is an all-purpose term meaning boss or supervisor. In America its usage is of twofold derivation: "Chief" as a title refers to the primary, elected or appointed leader of any group, i.e. Chief Justice, Chief Engineer, Chief Surgeon, Commander in Chief, etc. Colloquially, "Chief" is a generic term people have adopted for the leader of any native American tribal group.

Maurice is intentionally using irony to belittle Holden.

Page 101: "chisel me"

To be chiseled is to be gypped, swindled, taken advantage of, or cheated. Since the late 19th or early 20th century a "chiseler" has been a professional cheater, a con man.

Page 102: "wutchamacallit"

Whatever-you-might-call-it. A general noun for an unnamed, or unnamable thing. (See "**wuddayacallit** " Chapter 13, page 126, above)

Page 103/104: "pretending I had a bullet in my guts"

In the passage that follows Holden acts out a scene that would be very familiar to moviegoers in the 1940's. It's corny and Holden knows this, but the melodrama seems to suit the mood he's in. Imagining that he is enduring a painful, grave injury takes some of the sting out of Holden's recent humiliation at the hands of Maurice.

Page 104: "my automatic"

An automatic pistol fires bullets in rapid succession without the need to cock or reload between firings.

Page 104: "high-pitched, yellow-belly voice"

The squirrelly bad guy in the movies usually turned *yellow* (see **"...one of those very yellow guys"** page 109, Chapter 13) when the going got tough and began pitifully begging for mercy. Peter Lorre did that more than once; Elisha Cook Jr. was a thoroughly believable creep, too.

Chapter 15

(Sunday morning from "around ten o'clock" to noon.)

In which Holden has breakfast and discusses literature with an unlikely audience.

> We start to pet and that's when I get
> Her powder all over my vest.
> After I kind of straighten my tie
> She has to borrow my comb
> Its one kiss then we continue again
> Walking my baby back home
>
> > Walking My Baby Back Home,
> > Roy Turk, 1930

Page 105: "That was a long time ago."

Many readers find it hard to believe that just 19 hours earlier Holden was standing on Thomson Hill right next to the Revolutionary War cannon listening to the Pency / Saxon Hall football game.

Page 105: "Sally Hayes"

Sally has long been a common name in English song and legend. Generally, a girl who bears the name of Sally is uncomplicated, plain, loyal, and of the neighborhood. Sally's name haunts scores of traditional songs and nursery rhymes. A few of the most common are:

Sally Goodin
Little piece of pie, little piece of puddin'
I'm goin' down the road to see Sally Goodin
Goin' down the road, the road's a little muddy
So durn drunk I can't stand steady ...etc.

Oh, Sally
Oh, Sally, oh, Sally,
You know I've been good.
I carry your water
And I pack in your wood...etc.

Sally pops up in at least three sailors' work chanteys:

Sally

Oh Sally she's the gal that I love dearly...etc.
O, Sally Brown
I shipped on board of a Liverpool liner,
Way, ho, a-rolling go...etc.

Little Sally Rackett

Little Sally Racket
Haul 'er Away!
Pawned my favourite jacket
Haul 'er Away...etc.

Children's rhymes:

Little Sally Walker, sitting in a saucer, etc.

Old Sally Walker[47], Old Sally Glenn.
Old Sally Walker, choose young men...etc.

---

[47] Sometimes "Water" is substituted for "Walker".

Poetry:

> *Sally Gardens* (W. B. Yeats, 1889)

Folk song:

> *Down in My Sally's Garden*

American popular song:

> *Sally in Our Alley* (1750) Henry Carey
> *My Gal Sal* (1905) Paul Dresser[48]

There is no reason why Salinger (or Holden, for that matter) would not have been aware of most of these traditional lyrics. But Sally's popularity did not end with the early twentieth century. Post-forties appearances include:

> *Long Tall Sally*; Little Richard,1956
> *Mustang Sally*; Mack Rice 1965
> *Ride, Sally, Ride* and *Sally Can't Dance* ; Lou Reed, 1974
> *Lay Down, Sally*; Eric Clapton, 1977
> *Sally Sue Brown*: Bob Dylan (1987/88)

Literature:

Sally is the name of Charlie Brown's sister in the Peanuts comic strip and Dick's and Jane's sister in the popular school primer series from 1930 through 1965. Sally Phelps, sister of Tom Sawyer's Aunt Polly, appears in both The Adventures of Tom Sawyer and The Adventures of Huckleberry Finn by Mark

---

[48] Brother of Theodore Drieser, American novelist.

Twain. Sally is a character in both The Cat in the Hat by Dr. Seuss and The Mist by Stephen King.

Film:

Sally (1925), *Sally* (1929), *Sally* (1979), *Sally* (2000), *When Harry Met Sally* (1989).

Page 105: "Mary A Woodruff"

A fictitious girl's school.

Page 105: "necked"

In the olden days before birth control became common and reliable for women, sexual intercourse was not approached with the same degree of insouciance that it is today. Women, and especially girls, were expected to delay intimate sexual contact as long as possible in order to assess the degree to which a young man was "serious" about the relationship. Errors in judgment had serious and long-lasting consequences. The language of these times reflects the incremental way in which physical intimacy progressed by degrees from the formal introduction to "carnal knowledge"[49].

Terms like "spooning", "petting", "necking", and "fondling" had very real and specific connotations, even if there was no universal agreement as to precisely what each meant. "Necking", and its somewhat older sibling "spooning" were generally terms for passionate kissing. "Petting" and its somewhat more graphic sister "fondling" obviously included elements of physical contact below the neck. Even in the early 21st century such terms as "make out", "get with", and "scamming" have widely varied interpretations. (See **"...get to first base..."** Chapter 11)

---

[49] *Carnal knowledge* was a euphemism for sexual intercourse. It is rarely used today except in an ironic or joking way.

But, as the song reminds us, "a kiss is still a kiss".

Page 106: "rushing hell"

Romancing or wooing with intensity. This comes from the definition of "rush" as "to move forward with reckless impetuosity". When a girl (or a guy for that matter) is being pursued romantically she or he is being rushed.

Page 106: "clock at the Biltmore"

Now the Bank of America Plaza Building (Madison Avenue at 43rd Street), the Biltmore was one of New York's grandest old hotels. There was, at the entrance to its central court lounge, a wonderfully ornate, large, old clock. In the 19th century, before most ordinary people had wristwatches, decorative clocks were quite common on streets and in public buildings. While not as fabulous as the one at the Waldorf Astoria, the clock at the Biltmore hotel became the traditional meeting place downtown. All one had to say was "Meet you under the clock" and the rendezvous was set. Everyone knew where it was, and no tourist to New York could call his visit complete without having been there and seen it. The clock was

immortalized in the F. Scott Fitzgerald short story, "Under the Biltmore Clock".

Page 106: "pain in the ass"

An annoyance; also heard as "a pain in the neck". Not to be confused with the aforementioned "poker up the ass" (see Chapter 12, page 86, **"...poker up his ass..."**) which is quite a different problem.

Page 107: "Grand Central Station"

Quite the grandest train station in New York, and very possibly the world, Grand Central is actually a terminal since all trains stop there. The New York Central railroad built its first "Depot" near the site of the current Madison Square Garden in 1869. The Depot was moved to its current location in 1871 when "Grand Central", as it came to be

called, boasted as its centerpiece a massive 100 by 650 foot train shed. More impressive than London's Crystal Palace, this glass and steel structure was fronted by a wonderful facade, built in the classical style, which met travelers as they passed through the stone columns to the 16,000 square foot lobby. Impressive as it was, this travel complex was never capable of accommodating the number of trains and passengers required and at the turn of the century plans were already under way to create a new Grand Central Station at Park Avenue and 42nd

Street which, at the time, was not nearly as "gaudy, bawdy (or) naughty"[50] as the song was later to claim.

Nepotism, favoritism and good old-fashioned back-room chicanery resulted in two competing architectural firms, Reed and Stern of St. Paul, Minnesota and Warren and Wetmore of New York being awarded the construction contract as "associated architects". It took no less than six years of compromising, wrangling, hair-pulling and threats to reconcile and adapt their two competing visions into a single plan.

The new design for the terminal was modern, massive, innovative and fiscally shrewd. Since modern electric trains no longer required an open rail-yard, the entire terminal could be built underground, minimizing the amount of street level construction. During the ten-year duration of the project, in spite of the massive scale of the construction, trains continued to run through the old Terminal as well as a temporary one located a Lexington and 42nd Street. Once nearly three million cubic feet of Manhattan dirt had been removed and the terminal's operating structures confined below street level, the "air space" above was ready to be leased to developers at premium prices. The magnificent Beaux Arts structure initiated a frenzy of development in the immediate area. Grand office buildings and the 77 story Chrysler building followed shortly. By 1947 the Grand Central Terminal was the busiest train station in the country; more than 65 million visitors per year bustled in and out of this marvelous edifice.

The post-war period brought additional challenges to one of New York's most emblematic edifices. Even though the Terminal had been declared a protected landmark by the New York City Landmarks Preservation Commission in 1967, Penn Central, the conglomerate that owned the Grand Central complex, took the city to court in order to build a fifty-five story office building in place of the existing terminal entrance.

---

[50] Crooner/actor Dick Powell sang these words in the 1933 film, *42nd Street*.

The case, ultimately decided against Penn Central, went all the way to the U.S. Supreme Court.

After extensive renovations in 1994 by its new owner, Metro-North, Grand Central Station was returned to its 1913 glory. There are now several restaurants and more than fifty shops to service travelers and tourists who have come to view one of the most impressive relics of old New York.

Today's visitor enters the station through the new entrance at 43rd and Lexington and immediately encounters the vast main concourse. The half an acre of marble floor, lit from all sides by high windows, is daily crisscrossed by ten of thousands of visitors and commuters. The famous "sky ceiling" is lit by 59 stars in a representation of the night constellations over Manhattan. At the east end of this floor you will see the grand marble staircase featured in Brian de Palma's *The Untouchables* (1987) and other films. The mezzanine and lower levels are now given over almost entirely to eating establishments, shops, boutiques and the splendid Grand Central Market where one can pay the going rate for gourmet foods and delicacies. Vanderbilt Hall, which used to be the main waiting room, is located on the south side of the main concourse. At different times of the year this 12,000 square-foot space plays home to a wide variety of exhibits, craft fairs, public events and shows.

Page 108: "two nuns"

Up until the second Vatican Council (1962 through 1965) when many archaic restrictions were lifted, nuns of any order were expected to wear their designated church-authorized "habits" at all times. This made them very easy to spot. Now, of course, nuns may go out in public dressed much like everyone else, though they generally continue to keep their heads covered, their styles conservative and their colors muted.

Painting   by   Diego

Page 108: "Mark Cross"

If you had a lot of money and were willing to spend it on high-end leather goods, Mark Cross at Fifth Avenue and 26th Street (later 55th) was the place to go. Originally a Boston, Massachusetts-based company (1845), Mark Cross had established itself in New York by 1892 as a place where a gentleman could buy anything from a saddle to a billfold. Later they became purveyors of ladies handbags, desk accessories and all manner of leather items. For many years Chrysler's Fifth Avenue automobile was available with a Mark Cross luxury interior option package. Mark Cross is now owned by parent company Cross, Inc., manufacturers of Cross pens.

In a literary connection, ownership of the Mark Cross Company was acquired in 1892 for $6,000 by socialite/artist Gerald Murphy. Murphy, along with his wife Sara, were the European holiday hosts to F. Scott Fitzgerald, Ernest Hemingway, Noel Coward, Pablo Picasso and other luminaries

at their fabulous estate on the French Mediterranean coast, Villa America. They were famous for their parties and indulgent hospitality. Guests who enjoyed their visits commented on the Murphy's spontaneity and joie de vivre. In his posthumously published memoir A Moveable Feast, Hemingway portrayed them as predatory creatures consuming the very talent they surrounded themselves with, but by then he was well-known for turning on his friends after they'd been used up.

Page 108: "bourgeois"

A term originally used by the French to denote the upper classes of society, it has since come to stand for a provincial narrow-mindedness, materialism, hypocrisy, a dearth of cultural awareness and stubborn devotion to the status quo. Sinclair Lewis in his novel Babbitt (1922) created what will probably always remain the classic American bourgeois in George Follanbee Babbitt.

Early twentieth century author H.L. Mencken coined the term "boob-oisie" to collectively refer to what he saw as the vast, unsophisticated and frequently malicious majority.

Page 109: "Salvation Army...Christmas time ..."

The Salvation Army has a long tradition of stationing bell-ringers with donation kettles outside of stores and businesses at Christmas time.

Founded in London in 1865 by Methodist Minister William Booth, The Salvation Army took a quasi-military approach to evangelical Christianity. Officers wore uniforms and attained rank as they worked their way "up" toward, well, salvation. Though the mission of The Salvation Army was to "win the world for Jesus" it is not generally considered an autonomous creed or sect. The Army eschewed the sacraments of baptism, communion and marriage in order for its members to focus more intently upon God's grace. Members were expected to refrain from gambling, illicit drug use, alcoholic beverages and tobacco. The organization was open to both men and women, members were expected to actively participate in the work of the Army and divisions maintained brass bands that were often of very high quality.

Though considered marginal today (outside of its chain of Thrift-stores), The Salvation Army was, in its time, a powerful force for temperance and moral redemption. Initially devoted to rescuing drunks, drug addicts and prostitutes, the Army grew substantially in influence in the post-Civil War United States. Today they are best known for their skid row missions, meals provided to the homeless, and thrift stores, the profits from which are poured back into charitable and philanthropical causes.

Page 109: "little black book"

The book the nun is carrying could be the New Testament which is often published as a separate volume from the Old Testament, or a Concordance. The New Testament is the part of the Christian bible devoted to the life and teachings of Jesus of Nazareth, called Christ. The humorous irony here lies in the phrase "little black book" which is generally used to describe a bachelor's collection of women's names and telephone numbers.

Page 111: "Julius - "

Caesar, of course. One of Shakespeare's other tragedies. Spoiler alert: He is stabbed multiple times in Act III and dies.

Page 111: "Mercutio"

Juliet's cousin; Romeo's friend, he is made "worms-meat" of in Act III. Audiences are generally of two minds about Mercutio. Either he is a voluble wit whose energetic presence enlivens an already wonderful play, or he is a verbose narcissist whose overwrought bombast hobbles the narrative flow. Shakespeare clearly loved the fellow and wrote him elaborate flights of poetic philosophizing. Like it or not, his Queen Mab speech in Act I has given hams[51] everywhere an opportunity to chew on painted plywood street scenes.

Page 112: "...bit of old Ernest Morrow's mother..."

Do you remember the woman who rode the train from Trenton to Newark in Chapter 8? You have to wonder what commonalities Holden feels this woman – the one with all the "rocks" - shares with the nun.

Page 112: "...the National at Forest Hills..."

Forest Hills is in Queens, New York and hosts the U.S. Open tennis tournament, formerly called the National Championships. It has been home to the Westside Tennis Club since 1913. A private, planned community founded in 1908, Forest Hills has always been noted for its lovely homes, townhouses and apartments set in a park like, suburban setting.

Page 113: "blue"

Sad. To feel "blue" is to experience lingering sorrow. When someone has the "blues" they are sad.

The schizoid symbolism of the color blue gives those unfamiliar with Western culture the fits. On the one hand, blue can be lovely and optimistic if it is confined to skies, eyes, clothing or water. A blue ribbon is the first place award in a competition. Blue skies connote optimism and a sense of well-being. Blue eyes are romantic.

On the other hand blue, when applied to skin tone or mood, is not a good thing at all. Singing "the blues" refers to the

---

[51] A *ham* is a bad, though usually enthusiastic, actor.

sorrowful songs that grew out of African-American regional music. "Blue-haired" is a derisive term used on women of advanced age who try to brighten their grey hair with commercial "bluing". A "bluenose" is a humorless person who advocates a very rigid moral code. A "blue blood" is someone who belongs to a royal or particularly socially prominent family. "Blue-balls" is a painful (and apocryphal) over-stimulation of the male testes that must be relieved as soon as possible by orgasm. A "blue joke" is obscene. A "blue baby" is one born sickly and weak due to a heart defect. A "blue book" is either: a thin notebook in which essay exams are taken, a register of socially prominent persons, or a collection of specialized data or information as in the Kelly Blue Book of used automobile prices. A "blue-stocking" is a woman with pronounced literary or social pretensions. The phrase, "once in a blue moon" is used to describe an event that occurs infrequently. Blue skin is either bruised or necrotic.

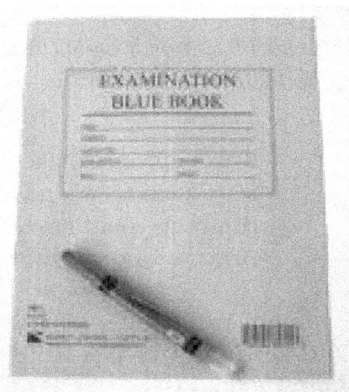

Chapter 16

(Sunday, December 10, 1949, around noon)

In which Holden finds an old recording, buys theater tickets and visits Central Park.

> Brush up your Shakespeare,
> Start quoting him now.
> Brush up your Shakespeare
> And the women you will wow...
> Cole Porter, 1948

Page 114: "...kissed her ass..."

When one flatters excessively it is referred to as "ass kissing". A commonly disparaged means of gaining favor or advantage with someone by excessively praising them, this phrase has all but replaced "toadying". People who do it are called "*brown noses*" for obvious reasons.

On the other hand, the command "kiss my ass" is used to inform someone of their worthlessness or inferiority. Neither of these expressions, while extremely common, ought to be used in polite conversation.

Page 114: "record"

In the earliest days of recorded sound, Thomas Edison devised a machine that could engrave audio vibrations upon a hard wax cylinder. The cylinder was turned on an arm while an electrified needle read and amplified the engraved vibrations. By 1890 these cylinders were capable of holding up to two minutes of recorded music. Between 1901 and 1908 both Victor and Columbia began marketing flat disk recordings engraved in the familiar, tight spiral fashion and that revolved clockwise as they were played. These recordings were designed to be spun at 78 rpm (revolutions per minute) and were capable of holding up to 10 minutes worth of music on each side. The term "record album" comes from this period. Since longer musical works, symphonies, operas, etc. required more than once disk to be played in their entirety, albums of stiff cardboard were created to hold the set of disks together in paper sleeves.

It was not until 1948 that "long play" (lp) vinyl recordings were capable of playing back up to 30+ minutes of music per side at a more moderate 33 1/3 rpm.

The record Holden has purchased for Phoebe is one of the 78 rpm disks. It would have been quite brittle as these records were pressed from an early plastic material similar to Bakelite, a popular synthetic of the 1930's and 40's. The paper sleeve protected the recordings from scratches, but did nothing to prevent fracture. These recordings were almost always black in color, though brick-red was an occasional novelty hue.

Page 114: "Little Shirley Beans"

There is no real recording of "Little Shirley Beans". The song is fictitious. The title does convey a sassy exuberance, however, and someone ought to get to work on it.

Page 114: "her front teeth were out"

Boys and girls lose their two front "baby" teeth at about seven and one-half years of age.

Holden (and Salinger) would certainly have been familiar with Spike Jones' recording of "All I Want For Christmas Is My Two Front Teeth" which made it to #1 on the popular music sales charts in 1949.

Everybody pauses and stares at me
These two teeth are gone as you can see
I don't know just who to blame for this catastrophe!
But my one wish on Christmas Eve is as plain as
it can be!
All I want for Christmas is my two front teeth
My two front teeth, see, my two front teeth?
Gee, if I could only have my two front teeth
Then I could wish you Merry Christmas.

It seems so long since I could say
"Sister Suzy Sitting on a thistle".
Every time I try to speak
All I do is whistle.
Don Gardner, 1946

Page 114/115: "Estelle Fletcher"

When it comes to identifying the inspiration behind the fictional singer *Estelle Fletcher*, many insist that it has to be the legendary "Lady Day", Billie Holiday (1915 - 1959). This, to me, seems unlikely. Holiday was essentially a balladeer with an inimitable approach to a lyric. She could certainly be "sassy" when she wanted to, but

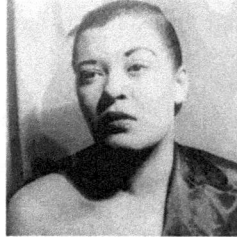

Billie Holiday

her best recordings were known more for their heart than sass.

160

A strong case can be made for *Ella Fitzgerald (1917-1996)*, whose initials, coincidentally, are also E.F. Ella was a much-

Ella Fitgerald

loved and greatly respected jazz singer through the last sixty years of the twentieth century. She could certainly sing "sassy" and "whorehouse" when she wanted to. Her charged, improvized "scat"[52] singing was the model to which others aspired. Her career, which began at 17, went officially stellar in 1938 with the release of "A-Tisket a-Tasket". The song was based on an old nursery rhyme, but in Ella's naughty interpretation it seemed to take on another life altogether.

> *A-tisket a-tasket*
> *A green-and-yellow basket*
> *I bought a basket for my mommie*
> *On the way I dropped it*
>
> *I dropped it, I dropped it*
> *Yes, on the way I dropped it*
> *A little girlie picked it up*
> *And put it in her pocket*
>
> *She was truckin' on down the avenue*
> *But not a single thing to do*
> *She went peck, peck, pecking all around*
> *When she spied it on the ground...*

---

[52] "Scat" is a term used to describe the rhythmic substitution of words or syllables in an improvised line of jazz, often in a "call-and-response" duet with other members of the band.

Although she did not make her Broadway debut (*St. Louis Woman*) until 1946, Pearl Bailey was well known to jazz connoisseurs through the 1940's. While stylistically she matches the description Holden gives us of Estelle Fletcher, to me she seems unlikely if only because she primarily confined herself to the Philadelphia and Washington, D.C. nightclub circuits in the 1930's and 40's and did little recording.

Pearl Bailey

Another likely candidate is Broadway star Ethel Waters who had been a New York fixture singing jazz in Harlem clubs since 1919.

Ethel Waters

She recorded for Black Swan records and toured with *Fletcher Henderson* and his orchestra. She signed a recording contract with the much larger Columbia Records in 1925. Ethel Waters' popular recordings were frequently jazz and be-bop, a variant. Sassy? You bet! The titles of some of her early recordings say it all: *"Take Your Black Bottom Outside", "Shoo Shoo Boogie Boo", "Second-Handed Man", "My Baby Sure Knows How To Love", "Long Lean Lanky Momma", "I Like The Way He Does It", "If You Don't Think I'll Do Sweet Pops (Just Try Me)", "Do What You Did Last Night", "Back Bitin' Mamma".*

(It isn't much of a stretch to get *Estelle* out of *Ethel,* take the *Fletcher* from bandleader/ arranger Henderson and arrive at the artist who sang "Little Shirley Beans".) In 1949, already a Broadway star, she was nominated for a Best Supporting Actress Academy Award for her performance in the film, *Pinky.* She received the New York Drama Critics Award in 1950.

Page 115: "Dixieland and whorehouse"

Dixieland is a jazz style developed in the early 1900's in, and inextricably associated with, *New Orleans,* Louisiana. The name "Dixie", which has for more than 150 years been synonymous with the American south, is of obscure provenance and unknown origins. The customary *Dixieland* ensemble included a drum set, trombone, clarinet, trumpet, banjo or guitar, and a string bass. The standard uniform has always included white trousers, a red and white striped jacket and a flat-topped straw

hat. Outside of hard-core fanatics, *Dixieland* is considered something of a musical novelty today.

Just as tenacious as the stories of presidents being born in log cabins has been the tradition among jazz singers and musicians, at least partly legendary, that really good jazz musicians got their start performing in houses of prostitution. The *whorehouse style* may generally be described as reckless, profane, boisterous, suggestive, and if not downright sloppy, a studied carelessness was the desired effect. There was an irresistible down-and-dirty aura about whorehouses that made them the ideal breeding ground for be-bop, blues and funk. Certainly whorehouses, at least the successful, upscale ones, did hire musicians and singers to entertain their clients, but many of these musicians performed just as often in church. Some would say that the practice of performing in the whorehouse on Saturday night and the church on Sunday morning became a common one. I don't think there is any question that the whorehouses compensated their performers better, but the church, by far, provided the more attentive and responsive audience.

Page 115: "Paramount... Astor... Strand...Capitol"

The names of Manhattan movie theaters.

Page 116: "five bucks for it"

Five dollars is awfully expensive for any kind of record in the 1940's when popular recordings commonly sold for 20 to 75 cents. Either the shopkeeper knew he had a rarity on hand, or he sized up his customer and made him pay dearly for what he wanted.

It is interesting to note that "five bucks" is also the price Holden had agreed to pay for a "throw" with Sunny in Chapter 13.

Page 116: "...Sunday...three shows playing..."

Theatre matinees are more common now than they were during the 1940's. A visitor to Manhattan today would have no problem finding lots of matinees available on a Sunday. Plays generally run eight shows a week; Tuesday through Sunday evenings and two matinees, one on Saturday and the other on either Wednesday or Thursday afternoon. Traditionally Mondays are "dark", meaning there is no performance. Oddly, there were no Sunday matinees for I Know My Love"

Page 116: "*I Know My Love*...the Lunts"

The play Holden has tickets for opened at the Shubert Theatre on Broadway in November of 1949 and closed in June, 1950 after 246 performances. The Shubert Theatre was, and continues to be, located at 225 West 44th Street just off Times Square. *"I Know My Love"* was what is termed a "drawing-room comedy"[53] and directed by Alfred Lunt.

Holden's attendance at this matinee unequivocally places the story in mid-December, 1949.

Broadway legends Alfred Lunt (1892-1977) and his wife Lynn Fontanne (1887 1983) reigned for more than fifty years as the king and queen of the American stage. Married in 1922 they are believed to have performed in anywhere from 25 to 40 plays together. Beginning with *A Young Man's Fancy* in 1919 and ending with a long run in *The Visit* (1957 - 1960) the couple known affectionately as "The Lunts" performed almost exclusively with each other. They acted in plays by authors as well-known, and diverse, as William Shakespeare, George Bernard Shaw, Noel Coward and Terrence Rattigan. Coward's play, *Design for Living* was written expressly for them.

Alfred Lunt was the winner of two Tony awards, an Emmy and was nominated for an Academy Award in the Best Actor category for *The Guardsman* in 1931. Lynn Fontanne was

---

[53] *Drawing-room comedy* is a term used to describe a particular kind of play, often set in a single room, where wealthy, class-conscious individuals exchange witty remarks with one another. It takes its name from the room in upper-class British homes where visitors were "entertained" by the host(s)..

nominated for an Academy Award (Best Actress) for the same film. The Lunts did little work in Hollywood; some television in the late 50's, and Lynn Fontanne did three motion pictures. They considered themselves to be stage performers and had little patience for the fragmented way in which screen performers worked. Their summer home *Ten Chimneys* in southeast Wisconsin, to which they retired every July and August, eventually became a haven for New York playwrights and actors. A U.S. 37 cent postage stamp was issued in the honor in 1999.

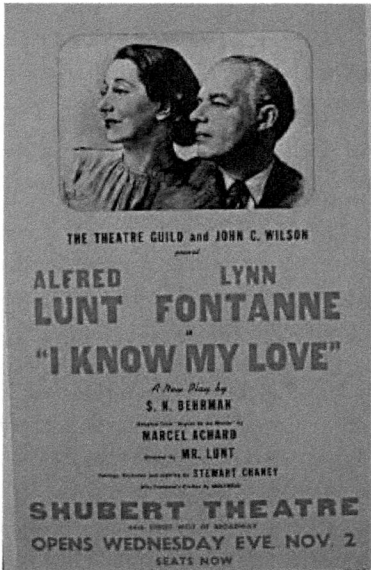

THE THEATRE GUILD and JOHN C. WILSON

ALFRED LUNT   LYNN FONTANNE

in

"I KNOW MY LOVE"

A New Play by
S. N. BEHRMAN

MARCEL ACHARD

MR. LUNT

STEWART CHANEY

SHUBERT THEATRE

OPENS WEDNESDAY EVE. NOV. 2
SEATS NOW

It is hard to think of a contemporary equivalent of the *Lunts*. Neither Broadway nor the institution of marriage is quite what it used to be and, as a consequence, a professional partnering of their remarkable longevity is all but out of the question today. Certainly husbands and wives have worked together in the theatre and in film, but nowhere near as exclusively or for as long as Alfred Lunt and Lynn Fontanne. Richard Burton and Elizabeth Taylor, who married each other twice, did some dramatic work on stage (notably Noel Coward's *Private Lives)* and several good films together, but each worked just as often independent of the other. In their later years the married couple Hume Cronyn and Jessica Tandy worked together on stage *(The Gin Game)* and in film *(Cocoon)* but, again, most of their best work was done apart. The comic duo of George Burns and Gracie Allen performed in vaudeville and, later, film for more than forty years. Neither was considered a dramatic actor until Burns, late in his career after the death of his wife, became successful in a series of film comedies. In a twenty year marriage Lucille Ball and Desi Arnaz played what were essentially the same characters through ten years worth of *"I Love Lucy"* and two films, *The Long, Long Trailer* (1954) and *Forever, Darling* (1956). Spencer Tracy and Katherine Hepburn were a scintillating screen couple, but never actually married each other. R2D2 and C3PO were droids.

Page 117: "Laurence Olivier"

Throughout a 60 career on stage and film Sir Laurence Olivier (knighted in 1947) secured ten Academy Award nominations, two honorary Oscars (1949 and 1979), six Emmy Awards, and three Golden Globe Awards. His presence on stage was regarded as electrifying, his voice thrilling. Though as a young leading man he was virile and handsome onscreen, he smoothly made the transition to character parts as he aged. His best film performances include, *King Lear, 1984; Marathon Man, 1976; Long Day's Journey into Night*, 1973; *The Entertainer*, 1960; *Henry V*, 1945; *That Hamilton Woman*, 1941; *Rebecca*, 1940; and *Wuthering Heights*, 1939. Olivier, never regarded by his peers as a great Shakespearean actor, was considered by some to be a ham. Still, his riveting film-version of *Hamlet* (1948) is another in the series of films that self-proclaimed movie-hater Holden tells us about in this novel.

J.D. Salinger met Olivier in England during the spring of 1952 while being shown around London by British publisher Hamish Hamilton. If Olivier was aware of the slights he had endured at the hands of Salinger's fictional creation he said nothing about it. In 1954 Olivier tried to secure the rights to do a BBC radio version of Salinger's story, "For Esme – With Love and Squalor", and was, of course, turned down.

Page 117: "...sad, screwed-up guy"

One of the earliest definitions for the expression "screwed-up" was *twisted,* or *fixed in a contorted position.* Consequently *screwed-up* has come to be an all-purpose term for *not as it should be; in bad shape.* A person who is screwed-up is a mess; damaged in some way, or mentally unbalanced. Holden seems to have made an accurate appraisal of Hamlet's personality, though he might just as well have been talking about himself.

Page 117: "Ophelia's brother"

Laertes (Lay-air-tees). He returns in Act 4 to seek vengeance on Hamlet for the death of his father, Polonius. Before he can implement his plan, he is emotionally poleaxed by Gertrude's story of Ophelia's drowning. His is one of the four corpses left littering the stage at the conclusion of Act V.

Page 117: "lot of advice"

One of the most famous and frequently quoted passages in all of Shakespeare is Act I Scene 3 of Hamlet in which Polonius, Ophelia's pompous and voluble father, advises his son Laertes prior to the young man's voyage to France:

> *Be thou familiar, but by no means vulgar;*
> *The friends thou hast, and their adoption tried,*
> *Grapple them to thy soul with hoops of steel;*
> *But do not dull thy palm with entertainment*
> *Of each new-hatch'd, unfledg'd comrade. Beware*

Of entrance to a quarrel, but, being in,
Bear 't that th' opposed may beware of thee.
Give every man thine ear, but few thy voice;
Take each man's censure, but reserve thy judgment...
Neither a borrower, nor a lender be;
For loan oft loses both itself and friend,
And borrowing dulls the edge of husbandry.
This above all: to thine own self be true,
And it must follow, as the night the day,
Thou canst not then be false to any man.

The ironic humor of this scene lies not in the quality of the advice, which is on the whole quite sound, but on the self-contradictory nature of any admonishment which so carefully stipulates all details of comportment while stressing that one must always be true to oneself. It is doubly ironic that this advice should come from a man who often acts in opposition to his own heeding and who is more than willing to be unscrupulous when such behavior is thought advantageous.

Page 117: "holster"

The leather holder for a knife is properly called a *scabbard* . A *holster* may hold either a pistol or a cell phone.

Page 118: "Mall...bandstand"

The Mall is the grand central promenade into Central Park. It is located just south of the *Bethesda Fountain* and north of the *Naumburg Bandshell*. *The Terrace Bridge*, the most elaborate architectural span in the park, lies between *The Mall* and *Bethesda Fountain*. By and large *The Mall* is the most active and populous gathering place in the park, and it is still popular with skaters, though today's skaters tend to be of the in-line or board variety.

The *Naumburg Bandshell* replaced the original cast-iron bandstand in 1922 as a gift from New York banker, Elkan Naumburg. Built of limestone in a neoclassical style this al fresco structure served from the day of its completion to 1969 as a gathering place for outdoor concerts provided by such diverse performing groups as John Philip Sousa, Duke Ellington, and the Grateful Dead. The Reverend Dr. Martin Luther King Jr. spoke there in the mid 1960's and it was the site of John Lennon's public funeral services. Since the 1980's the more popular events have been moved to the larger *Rumsey Playfield*.

Page 118: "We went last Saturday..."

It was not unusual at this time for children to attend school-sponsored field trips on Saturdays. It was considered a good way for city kids to get out of their apartments and experience the many cultural resources the city had to offer and the more progressive schools made a point of exposing their students to Manhattan's cultural treasures as often as possible

Page 119: "...the one where the pictures are, or the one where the Indians are?"

The Metropolitain Museum of Art is located just inside the park at East 82nd Street. That is "where the pictures are". The Indians, or at least life-size representations of them, are to be found at the *American Museum of Natural History* (see photo) on 79th Street between Central Park West and Columbus.

Page 119: "...tightening her skate...skate key"

A *skate key* was an essential tool which allowed shoe-skates to be adjusted and fastened to the soles of shoes. Children often wore one on a shoestring around the neck as a kind of playground talisman. The skate key looked much like any other key and served the double function of tightening the sizing lock on the base of the skate and the sole-gripping flange at the front.

It is very likely that you have never seen a *clamp-on shoe skate*. These were a popular and relatively inexpensive piece of recreational equipment for children in the 1930's through the early nineteen sixties. Made of nickel-plated or polished steel

right down to the wheels, each skate had an adjustable, sliding central last between the heel and toe pieces in order to accommodate shoes of different sizes. A screw underneath held the front and back of the skate rigid once the proper length had been achieved. The skate was then fixed to the shoe by means of a strap at the heel which buckled over the arch of the foot and two metal flanges that gripped the sole on either side of the ball of the foot and were tightened with a skate key. In order for these skates to be worn it was necessary to have shoes with a sewn-on sole; tennis shoes would not work for most clamp-on skates. Later, some more expensive models were made with a steel cap at the toe which permitted the wearing of shoes which did not have a sole to grip.

Metal skate wheels were easily jammed by even the smallest pieces of gravel and prone to slip out from under you on fast turns. The knees of boys' trousers were usually tattered from falls and girls, who wore dresses in those days, often sported knobby scabs below their hemlines.

If you were skating everyone within earshot knew it.

The steel wheels created a racket on the sidewalk like a dozen cheap tambourines thrown down stairs. The clamor is easily recalled by anyone old enough to remember the Eisenhower presidency.

In addition to their economy, clamp-on skates were remarkable versatile. By separating the front part of the skate from the back and nailing the two sections to opposite ends of a 18 inch chunk of two-by-four you could, in as matter of minutes turn one pair of skates into two "scooters", primitive precursors of the modern skateboard.

Clamp-on skates were very democratic; all but the very poorest children had access to a pair. One pair could be adjusted to fit any number of children, so they were commonly shared. Shoe skates, on which a high-topped lace-up was structurally fastened to the wheel assembly, were for "rich kids". At skating arenas and neighborhood indoor rinks the skates came equipped with hardwood wheels. Eventually composition wheels brought stability, a quieter ride and imperviousness to skating surface imperfections. These came to dominate the recreational market, but led inadvertently (and here I shudder) to roller disco, a popular and appalling misdemeanor of the 1970's.

Today skate-keys like the one Holden used are sold as nostalgic curiosities on e-bay.

Page 119: "Museum of Natural History"

The *American Museum of Natural History* at 79th Street and Central Park West is one of the cultural landmarks of Manhattan and visited by thousands each year. Though founded in 1869, construction did not begin on the present building until 1874. Over the decades the museum expanded its buildings through several phases, each under the supervision of a different architect. The result is a mélange of neo-gothic, classical and neo-Romanesque structural elements.

The Museum is well known for its displays of habitat groups; collections of preserved American species posed in lifelike, realistic settings. Holden refers to these in **Chapter 16** when he talks about the "deers...drinking out of that water hole" and the birds "stuffed and hung up on wires". The Museum's anthropological collections have long been considered outstanding. The tableaux of the Eskimo fishing and the squaw weaving a blanket would be found in these halls.

The *Hayden Planetarium* is located in an adjacent building.

Page 120: "this long, long Indian war canoe"

The American Museum of Natural History's collection includes a 62-foot Haida canoe from the American Pacific Northwest. Elaborately carved and painted it is easily as long as "three goddam Cadillacs in a row".

Page 121: "bosom"

A woman's chest is her *bosom*. A man can be said to have a bosom as well. Sometimes the word is pluralized when referring to female breasts. Holden's use of this term is both quaint and childlike. Not since the Victorian era has *bosom* been synonymous with *breasts*. Today the term *bosom* is never clinical, but has since the beginning of the twentieth century been used almost exclusively in reference to the seat of emotions or as the locus of social and familial attachments. That is, one's blood-pumping heart is located in the *chest cavity* while one's affectionate heart is located within one's *bosom*.

Page 121: "scarlet fever"

Scarlet Fever is caused by one of the various strains of the **streptococcus bacterium** (Streptococcus pyogenes). Usually the sufferer exhibits a fine, red rash over the surface of the upper body with a "strawberry" tongue to match, hence the designation "scarlet". Usually these symptoms are accompanied by a sore throat and, of course, a high fever. It is common for the skin to peel after recovery.

Strep bacteria are easily spread by the expulsion of microscopic droplets through coughing or sneezing. Prior to the advent of antibiotics Scarlet Fever was far more serious and debilitating than it is today. Children in the 19th century could spend weeks recuperating from a bout with this illness. Mutation of the virus into less potent strains has resulted in a modern illness known as *Scarlatina* which, while unpleasant, is relatively benign.

Page 122: "gasoline rainbows"

This commonly observed effect is the result of the way light refracts from a thin film of gasoline as it floats on the surface of water. Gasoline, which is lighter, floats on the surface in a film the variable thickness of which is only a few light wavelengths. Depending on the angle from which you are viewing, and the thinness of the gasoline film, you will see the refracted colors of the rainbow reflected off of the surface. The color you see depends on the thickness of the film in any particular spot.

Page 122: "...gay as hell..."

Holden means "as happy as one could imagine". Originally the English word *gay* meant happy or carefree. It wasn't until the nineteenth century that it acquired a sexual connotation, and it wasn't until the early twentieth century that the interpretation found its way into written English.

"As hell" is a common modifier used to mean "in the extreme".

It may sound hard to believe, but there was a time not so long ago when the word *gay* could mean either lighthearted or homosexual and there was almost never an occasion when it wasn't clear which you meant when using the word. Think about *The Flintstones*. In the 1960's their theme song declared that they were having "a gay old time" and not even conservative Christians bothered to protest. It never occurred to anyone that Fred and Barney were anything other than Neanderthal neighbors. (But I did have one friend who was convinced that Betty and Wilma , as the song professed, "had a secret love.")

Cornilia Otis Skinner's novel, *Our Hearts Were Young and Gay* was made into a film in 1944. Of course everyone who has ever been to an elementary holiday pageant knows how

thoroughly convulsed a bunch of fifth graders can become over the lyric, "now we don our gay apparel" from *Deck the Halls*. The period just before the turn of the 20th century was commonly referred to as "the gay nineties". Even today one can occasionally hear a reference to "gay Paree" (think: Paris).

Up until the 1950's Gay (or Gaye) was a popular girl's name.

The shortest street name in Greenwich Village is Gay.

Again, any time Holden uses a word or phrase suggestive of homosexuality it ads fuel to the interpretive fire of the "gay odyssey" explicators.

Chapter 17

(Sunday afternoon, December 18, 1949)

In which Holden meets Sally, sees the Lunts act light comedy, goes ice-skating at Radio City, and makes an unexpected proposal.

> I've got a feeling
> This year's for me and you
> So happy Christmas
> I love you baby
> I can see a better time
> When all our dreams come true
>> Fairytale of New York, by Jen Finer and Shane
>> MacGowan; recorded by the Pogues,

Page 123: "girls with their legs crossed"

This passage was almost certainly influenced by Irwin Shaw's frequently anthologized short story *Girls in Their Summer Dresses* (1938). Shaw was twenty-five when he wrote this bittersweet tale of urban marital ennui. One symptom of the marriage's fragile equilibrium is the husband's on-going interest in other women, symbolized by his fascination with girls and their legs.

Page 123: "bitches"

For at least the last five hundred years "bitch' has been used to identify a lewd, malicious or treacherous woman. The *Oxford English Dictionary* cites the first known use in literature from about 1400, "Whom calleste thou queine, skabde biche?"

("Who calls you queen, scabbed bitch?"). Ouch! Now that's really harsh.

In modern usage it seems to have become the all-purpose pejorative for a woman who holds an opinion contrary to one's own. If you were a rap artist in the 80's or 90's it included all women with the possible exception of your own mother.

Page 123: "very mean"

In Britain, "*mean*" means cheap, stingy, or parsimonious. In America it means cruel, harsh, or strict.

Page 123: "whistle better than anybody"

Whistling seems to be terribly important to Holden. Stradlater is terrible at it, but Harris Macklin is a regular Paganini of the pucker.

Whistling is a traditional antidote to fear, as in the expression "whistling in the dark". One whistles out of a false bravado designed as much to fool oneself as one's company. Or, as Oscar Hammerstein II put it, "I whistle a happy tune / and every single time / the happiness in the tune / convinces me that I'm not afraid".

The Whistler was an immensely popular radio program broadcast via the Columbia Broadcasting System (CBS) from 1942 through 1955. Each of the nearly 700 weekly episodes opened with the whistler's haunting melody behind an ominous narration of "I am the Whistler, and I know many things, for I walk by night..." An anthology, each week's episode was a self-contained tale of crime or mystery that commonly ended on an ironic, unexpected note. The opening melody, a melancholy series of ascending tones spanned two octaves and was considered quite difficult for whistlers to execute. Unable to find Harris Macklin, directors Sherman Marks and Sterling Tracy had to settle for the talents of Dorothy Roberts who faithfully, and musically, blew the tune for 13 years.

Page 124: "Tin Roof blues"

Because the earliest jazz composers were improvisational musicians who often didn't bother to document their work, controversy clouds the origins of many tunes, riffs, terms and stylistic embellishments. At least five different composers are given credit for *Tin Roof Blues* including George Brunis, Buddy Petit, Walter Melrose with the New Orleans Rhythm Kings, Paul J. Mares and Jellyroll Morton. Much of the confusion seems to stem from the fact the *Tin Roof Blues* sounds a lot like other blues melodies of the time. One of the most credible versions of the musical evolution of *Tin Roof Blues* holds that a theme originated by cornetist Buddy Petit was incorporated into a blues piece called *Rusty Nail Blues* by trombonist George Brunis. The New Orleans Rhythm Kings heard the piece, liked it, and bought the rights for $500. By the time they got around to recording the tune it was called *Tin Roof Blues* (1923) and Walter Melrose took credit for it. In another story Richard Jones is credited with its authorship and a different title, *Jazzin' Baby Blues* (1923). The same melody was re-recorded with different lyrics in 1953 (Kay Star) and 1954 (Jo Stafford) as *"Make Love to Me"*, though by this time there were eight individuals listed as composers.

> *I have seen, the bright lights burning up and down*
> *old Broadway,*
> *Seen 'em in gay[54] Havana, Birmingham,*
> *Alabama, and say,*

---

[54] See note: Page 174: **"...gay as hell..."** (Chapter 16)

they just can't compare with my hometown New
Orleans...

Page 124: "black coat...black beret"

The color black and the beret itself had become by the late forties part of the uniform of "beat generation" youth, both male and female. While Holden's story and characters may be just a bit early to have had any awareness of the growing Greenwich Village coffee house scene it is interesting that the utterly conventional Jane has adopted a look so suggestive of the 'beat' avant garde.

The social, musical and literary phenomena known as "the beat era" while having little impact upon Holden Caulfield, Jane and Sally nevertheless deserves mention at this point if only for its Manhattan roots and Greenwich Village / Columbia University genesis. It is assumed to have begun in 1944 when Allen Ginsberg, Neal Cassady, and Jack Kerouac met in the bookstores and coffee houses surrounding Columbia University. Shortly thereafter William S. Burroughs and Herbert Huncke, denizens of an increasingly drug and prostitution oriented Times Square, and Gregory Corso of Greenwich village joined the generally unkempt band of writers and social critics. By 1948 Kerouac had coined the term "beat generation" to describe people like himself and his friends; fatigued, resigned, disaffected, disappointed, and disillusioned. In many respects the devotees of the "beat" philosophy shared much in common with those Gertrude Stein had called the "lost generation"[55] of the 1920's and the "flower children" of the sixties, equal measures of adolescent idealism, cynicism, a passionately indignant response to wartime savagery; sexual re-evaluation; a weakness for consciousness-altering substances; a middle and upper-middle class, largely-white, urban following; and alignment with a particularly revolutionary musical style.

---

[55] A term she claimed to have borrowed from a French automobile mechanic.

The "beat" poets and writers drew inspiration from smoky coffee bars in Greenwich Village where Zen Buddhism was loudly discussed over the eccentric bleats of be-bop jazz musicians like Dizzy Gillespie, Charlie Parker and Miles Davis. Jazz patois altered the language. Bohemian attire inspired by habitués of Place Pigalle was du rigeur. The goatee, a chin beard often paired with a mustache, was adopted by most "hep-cats" (but very few "chicks", thankfully). Badly worn turtleneck

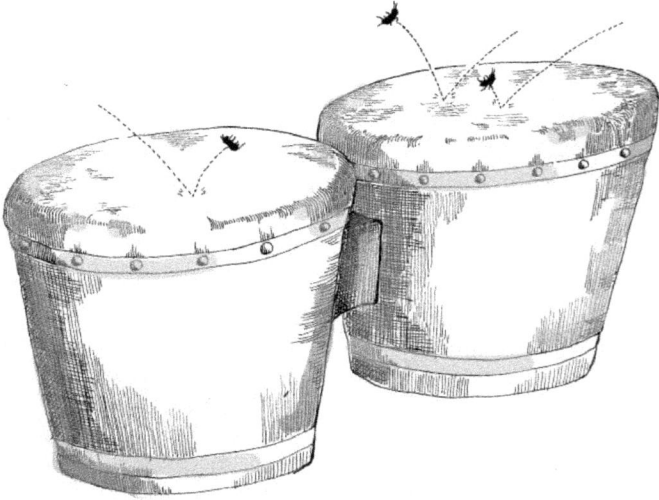

sweaters and slim, "pegged" trousers were "cool". The beret was considered "groovy", if not essential, headwear and black was the new…well, *black*. A dour, slightly pained expression on the outside was deemed sufficiently reflective of the angst within. Since this was the forties everyone smoked cigarettes prodigiously.

Musical instruments of choice were the saxophone, flute and "bongos", small hand-drums usually paired and played while gripped between the knees. Art was abstract. Radio, and later television, was hopelessly bourgeois. Popular forms of entertainment consisted of deep discussions, philosophical arguments and French and Italian "art" films.

By 1950 the locus of the *beat movement* had officially moved as far west as possible, to San Francisco. It wasn't until 1958 that San Francisco Chronicle columnist Herb Caen created the designation "beatnik", the "-ik" suffix suggestive of both Yiddish slang and certain Russian nouns.

So what became of the Beats? Other than defining a sub-genre of poetry they had very little lasting literary influence. Kerouac's *On The Road* is virtually the only beat prose still read today. A comic "type" they joined hillbillies, Chicago gangsters and dumb blondes in radio and television writers' rolodex of droll caricatures.

In reality they became older, more socially conventional and, both literally and figuratively, gave birth to the "hippies" of the 1960's.

Page 124/125: "Saturday Evening Post"

For more than forty years *The Saturday Evening Post* was the best-known popular magazine featuring short fiction by both new and established American writers. *The Saturday Evening Post* was first published in 1821 as a four-page weekly newspaper. Under the editorship of George Rex Graham the publication was promoted as "A Family Newspaper, Neutral in Politics, Devoted to Morality, Pure Literature, Foreign and Domestic News, Agriculture, the Commercial Interests, Science, Art, and Amusement". In 1899 a redesigned Saturday Evening Post was published as a weekly journal with a new editor, George Horace Lorimer. Lorimer almost single-handedly made the *Post* into an American literary institution. He not only sought out and published respected American writers like Theodore Dreiser, Frank Norris, Willa Cather, Jack London, Sinclair Lewis and Stephen Crane, but in 1916 he commissioned a series of cover illustrations from a 22

year-old Norman Rockwell. Over the next 45 years Rockwell's cover art would become significant as a reflection of an idealized collective American consciousness.

From the 1920's through the 1940's having a story published in the Saturday Evening Post became not only a great way for young writers like Irwin Shaw and F. Scott Fitzgerald to debut, but a reliable paycheck for established writers like Dreiser and London. J.D. Salinger placed one short story with the *Saturday Evening Post* prior to his service in W.W. II.

In the mid-1960's when virtually all American institutions were trying desperately to re-imagine themselves the *Saturday Evening Post*, already having severely cut back on its fiction content, severed its relationship with Norman Rockwell. By 1969 it had published its last issue.

Page 125: "horsed around"

In chapter 5 Holden is "horsing around" with some Pency Prep schoolmates after dinner (See Chapter 5, **Page 35: "...horsing around..."**). However, here he is engaging in an entirely different sort of play with Sally. Holden and Sally are *necking* (see Chapter 15 **Page 105: "necked"**), *petting* and, perhaps, *fondling*.

Page 125: "big clinch"

This *clinch* is a passionate embrace. In wrestling a "clinch" is used to describe a situation where the two combatants have locked one another in offensive holds.

Page 126: "jerks"

"Jerks" are fools, annoyances, people of no importance.

On the other hand, in the 19th century when drug stores had soda fountains (see Chapter 18, page 191 **"...went in this drugstore..."** below), young men were commonly hired to pull on long handles that dispensed carbonated water, tonic and seltzer much as a bartender will today draw a beer from a tap. These men who "jerked soda' came to be called "soda jerks". Popular wisdom had it that these young men spent most of their time idly chatting and flirting with young girls. By the

1930's the term "jerk" had come to signify any person who was idle, shiftless or of little importance.

Contrary to popular belief, the term is not a shortening of "jerk off", a euphemism for masturbation and denigrating label for any useless or unimportant person. Jerks were "jerks" long before they were chronic onanists.

Page 126: "dopey"

Stupid; foolish; pointless. Since the mid-19th century Americans have used the slang word *dope* to refer to a stupid person. The term comes from "dope" as slang for an illicit drug like heroin, opium, marijuana or any of their derivatives. A person drugged out of their senses was "doped" or "doped up" or a "dope-head", eventually "dopey". (See Chapter 12, **Page 85: "dope fiend"**)

In Walt Disney's 1937 animated film classic, *Snow White and the Seven Dwarfs,* the speechless dwarf who is both childlike and inept is named "Dopey".

Page 127: "big soul kiss"

This is an open-mouthed kiss, usually involving the tongue; what Americans call a French kiss. Holden is being sarcastic.

Page 127: "buddyroos"

Drunken or baby-talk for "buddy" or "friend".

Page 128: "very phony, Ivy League voices..."

The affected, drawn-out whine of the Ivy-league "privileged" class was once a stock dialect for any stage or television comic. Hallmarks of this vocal technique include a rigid, sometimes protruding jaw, flat vowels and sound emanating from the back of the throat. The late Jim Backus did a fine version of this on *Gilligan's Island* (CBS television 1964-67). Backus' character, Thurston Howell III, was a millionaire Harvard grad almost always seen in a blue blazer and yachting cap. Backus' characterization was largely drawn from an earlier persona, Hubert Updike, III. Before that, on *The Many Loves of Dobie Gillis* (CBS television 1960-63), actor Steve Franken adopted many of the same vocal mannerisms playing the character Chatsworth Osborne, Jr.

Page 128: "ice-skating at Radio city"

Under construction during the worst social and economic crisis America has yet faced, the Rockefeller Center was intended to be the first business complex to combine commercial, retail and entertainment elements within a titanic unified composition. The original thirteen structural components were designed with an eye toward aesthetic consistency; simple, geometric shapes emphasizing vertical lines. All buildings were faced with grey limestone.

The first of the Rockefeller Center's initial buildings to be completed was Radio City Music Hall. At just short of 6,000 seats it was the largest indoor theatre in the world when it opened in 1932. Upon the completion of the original complex in 1940, Rockefeller Center was praised as one of the best examples of 20th century urban architecture. The Radio City Music Hall came very close to being razed in the 1980's, but eventually received historic landmark status and was completely renovated in the 90's.

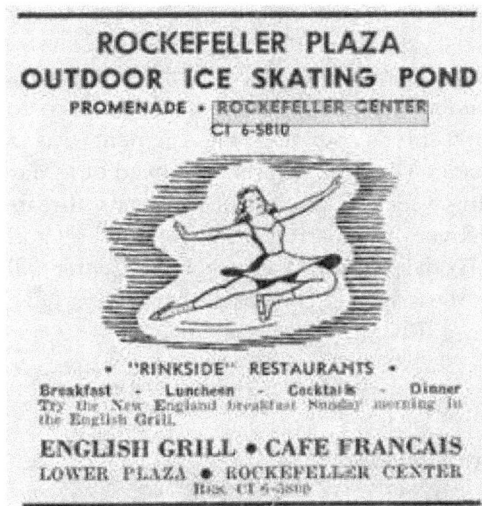

ROCKEFELLER PLAZA
OUTDOOR ICE SKATING POND
PROMENADE • ROCKEFELLER CENTER
CI 6-5810

• "RINKSIDE" RESTAURANTS •
Breakfast - Luncheon - Cocktails - Dinner
Try the New England breakfast Sunday morning in the English Grill.
ENGLISH GRILL • CAFE FRANCAIS
LOWER PLAZA • ROCKEFELLER CENTER
Res. CI 6-5800

Originally there wasn't much reason for anyone to enter the lower plaza in front of the RCA building (now the General Electric building). A large, dull, impersonal space, it served as an entrance to struggling and/or failing under-ground shops. At the height of the Great Depression John D. Rockefeller hired M.C. Carpenter of Cleveland, Ohio to install his newly patented system for making outdoor ice surfaces. On Christmas Day, 1936, the Radio City outdoor ice rink was inaugurated. Since then the skating rink has become a cherished winter tradition for locals and tourists alike. The annual opening of the ice rink, along with the lighting of the enormous Rockefeller Center Christmas tree, marks the beginning of the holiday season in New York.[56]

It is worth noting that one of the 20th century's most infamous art controversies occurred at Rockefeller Center after his wife, Abby Aldrich, convinced John D. Rockefeller to commission a mural by Mexican artist Diego Rivera. Rivera, a devoted socialist, set to work on a 63 foot celebration of workers in the modern world caught at the intersection of socialism, capitalism, science and industry. Though the mural in itself was guaranteed to engender controversy, most distressing to Rockefeller and the Center's building management was a depiction of Soviet leader Vladimir Lenin at the head of a May Day parade. Following weeks of fruitless negotiations, threats and counter-threats, Rivera was barred from the building and the mural destroyed. Today, a visitor to Rockefeller Center will find a mural by Jose Maria Sert in the space that was to have been occupied by Rivera's masterpiece.

**styled for Action
... over the counter
and on the rink!**

Page 129: "blue butt-twitcher of a dress"

Sally is wearing a short, pleated wool skirt common to recreational ice-skating. The idea of renting a skirt to go with your ice skates may seen odd to most readers, but it reminds us that proper attire was more important to New Yorkers of the forties than it is to, say, residents of Los Angeles in the 2000's. Many people today balk at the idea of

Bonny's.

New
"Princess"
Styling

Write
for
brochure.

Skating Skirts

---

[56] An interesting note pertaining to 1949: In that year the tree at Rockefeller Center was an enormous silver-painted spruce decorated with pastel lights and plastic revolving stars. On December 19th it caused a traffic jam that lasted for hours.

having to "dress up" for dinner or religious services even when the term "dress up" means nothing more than a clean T-shirt, shoes and socks. In Holden's era one always played tennis in "whites", a polo shirt was really for polo, rubber-soled shoes were strictly for the basketball or tennis court, and the T-shirt was underwear. That a girl like Sally would need a proper skirt for ice-skating was not at all unusual, but leaves unanswered the obvious question, would she also rent proper panties for such an activity – a disturbing concept in itself – or operate on the assumption that other skaters and observers needed to know what day of the week it was?

Page 129: "rubbernecks"

Rubbernecks or rubberneckers are gawkers; nosey people.

Page 130: "trim the tree Christmas Eve?"

In olden days it was common in many families to save the decoration of the Christmas tree for the night before Christmas. Finding the tree decorated on Christmas morning was for many children the first and most visually spectacular evidence of Santa Claus' miraculous visit. Today, however, it is not entirely unusual to find the Christmas tree decorated before the Halloween pumpkin has had a chance to grow grey fuzz.

Page 130: "guys fitting your pants all the time at Brooks"

Holden is referring to the indignities one endures while having a pair of pants fitted. A young man of Holden's class and status did not buy trousers "off-the-rack". It was necessary to go to a tailor for a proper fitting. This fitting included not only waist and inseam measurement, but *seat* allowances for a larger or smaller-than-average butt and a custom adjustment referred to as "dressing" right or left which provided an extra bit of room at the top of whichever pant leg the penis would generally fall. (I'm perfectly serious.) It is little wonder Holden had reservations about a process that required that level of physical intimacy.

Brooks Brothers Clothiers was, and continues to be, a purveyor of high-quality men's apparel. Holden would have been familiar with either their flagship store at 346 Madison Avenue or the smaller one at 5th Avenue and 53rd Street.

Page 131: "Book of the Month Club"

Founded in 1926, the year after *The Great Gatsby* was published, *The Book-of-the-Month Club* (BOMC) is the mother of all membership book clubs. Beginning as a service for readers who did not live near a full-service bookstore, the club gradually evolved into an American institution that has survived into the Amazon era.

Each month members would receive a newsletter promoting the featured selection as well as several alternate titles.

Brooks Brothers first store on Catherine Street.

requesting an alternate title or no book at all. In pre-Oprah times, selection by *The Book-of-the-Month Club* was a tremendous coup, virtually guaranteeing tens of thousands in sales. For an author's first novel to be selected was very rare.

In the summer of 1951 *The Catcher in the Rye* was the summer selection of the *Book-of-the-Month Club*. William Maxwell, editor of the New Yorker, was asked by the editors of the *BOMC* member newsletter *Book-of-the-Month Club News* to conduct an interview with the author. It was to be the only prepublication interview Salinger would permit.

Page 133: "oodles"

A whole lot; plenty; abundance. American slang since at least 1850.

Page 133: "dame breaking a bottle over a ship"

Ships are commonly christened by breaking a bottle of champagne over the bow. This practice began with the British navy in the late 17th century, but is essentially a modification of the ritual sacrifices to the gods with which ancient Greeks and Babylonians launched their sea-faring craft. It is customary for the christener to be a woman of some renown; in the forties that meant a queen, a president's, governor's or mayor's wife, an actress or a singer. As you might imagine, World War II brought about an increase in military ship production to the point where the christening of an important naval vessel occurred twice each day during 1943. There is no shortage of newsreel footage of these events since they were happy occasions and amusing mishaps were common.

A title of honor in Britain, the term "dame" is American slang; a mildly disrespectful – and archaic - synonym for *woman*.

Page 133: "chimpanzee riding a goddam bicycle with pants on"

First of all, it is the chimpanzee (pan troglodytes) wearing the pants, not the bicycle. Secondly, regardless of what Holden or anyone else may think there is simply nothing in the world more entertaining than watching a chimpanzee ride a bike.

Editor-in-Chief at Lit. Happens Publishing.

Page 133: "hit the ceiling"

To "hit the ceiling" is to get really angry; fly into a rage.

Chapter 18

(Sunday after 4:00 PM)

In which Holden eats a sandwich and goes to see a movie at Radio City.

> Sing, choirs of angels
> Sing in exultation
> Sing all ye citizens of heaven above.
>   John F. Wade, 1743

Page 135: "went in this drugstore and had a Swiss cheese sandwich"

Drugstores since the 19th century commonly had soda fountains and lunch counters. The lunch counter was a long, narrow metal or formica-covered surface about 18 to 24 inches wide raised above the level of the floor so that customers had to sit on high stools. The waitresses - and they were nearly always women - worked on one side of the counter between the kitchen and the customer, and the diner sat on the other. Service was quick and efficient because the distance from the counter to the kitchen was never more than a few feet. In an era before the invention of "fast food", this was one quick way to have a bite and be on your way.

Page 135: "Al Pike"

A joke; two jokes actually. A *pike* is a diving position wherein the torso is bent forward over the fully extended legs. Al fancies himself a diver (see **"half-gainer"** below).

In chapter 4 of F. Scott Fitzgerald's ***The Great Gatsby*** (see note below on **"The Great Gatsby"**, Chapter 18) Nick Carraway, our narrator, introduces us to some of the guests at one of Gatsby's opulent parties. In a scherzo of Dickensian whimsy, Fitzgerald has given them all silly names from the animal and vegetable world or otherwise goofy ones like *Smirke, Swett, Chrome* and *Bunsen*. Among them are those with fishing names: *Hammerhead, Beluga, Fishguard,* and *Snell*. Pike (a long, freshwater, bony fish) would fit right in with this crowd.

Page 135: "Choate"

Now Choate Rosemary Hall in Wallingford, Connecticut, Choate Academy was founded in 1900 as a boy's school to compliment Rosemary Hall, founded 1890, which was exclusively female. The two schools merged in 1974 to form a co-ed institution.

Page 135: "white Lastex...swimming trunks"

In the early years of the twentieth century bathing suits were made of loose, worsted wool and covered a great deal of the body. After World War I bathing suits began to shrink for both sexes and fit more closely. At about the same time new synthetic fabrics were being developed which would make innovative designs possible. Lastex was the trademark name for the first synthetic fiber to be used in the manufacture of newer style swimsuits. *Lastex* yarn was made by wrapping silk, nylon or rayon threads around an elastic *Latex* core. *Lastex* is not be be confused with *Spandex* which would, especially in the color white, have created a bathing suit of such near transparency as to render it unacceptable to all but the most exhibitionistic men.

Page 135: "half gainer"

This is a competitive dive in which the athlete springs from the board facing forward, rotates backward in the air in a half backward somersault, and enters the water headfirst, facing the board. A full gainer is one in which the diver leaves the board facing forward, does a back somersault, and enters the water feet first.

Actress Janet Gaynor won an Academy Award for Best Actress in 1928 for her performances in *Seventh Heaven, Sunrise* and *Street Angel.*

A Rogaine-er is another thing entirely.

Page 135: "inferiority complex"

Popularly, the term *inferiority complex* is used to describe a set of repressed beliefs that result in compensatory behaviors. Typically the subject's belief that he is inferior and/or inadequate results in boasting, risk-taking, interpersonal aggression and inappropriate displays of prowess.[57] Simply put, you think you are pathetic and habitually seek to try different ways to prove that is not true. A real *inferiority complex* (also called a *Napoleon complex*) results from the perception that one

---

[57] Of course there are a great many people whose only encounter with this term was "The Inferiority Complex" episode of I Love Lucy originally broadcast on February 2, 1953. In this episode, Ricky resorts to hiring a "physio-chiatrist" in an effort to convince Lucy that she really isn't "a big fat flop!" after all. Que chistoso!

is physically inferior to others. As described by Alfred Adler (1870-1937), perceived physical limitations could lead people to consider themselves less important or capable than others. For some this is a conscious process, for others unconsciousSome sociologists have used this theory to explain the successes of racial minorities and immigrants.

Page 136: "Carl Luce"

Holden's condescending, intellectual friend Carl carries, not accidentally, the same illustrious last name as publisher Henry Robinson Luce and his more famous wife, Clare Booth. Clare Booth Luce is one of those curious public figures whose name is a household word for decades then fades almost instantly into obscurity. Clare Booth Luce (1903-1987) was, among many accomplishments, a successful writer, a political activist and a diplomat. She was awarded the Presidential Medal of Freedom by Ronald Reagan in 1983.

Page 136: "Wicker Bar on 54th

Holden says that the *Wicker Bar* is on 54th Street in the "sort of swanky" *Seton Hotel*. This isn't possible. Today the *Seton Hotel* promotes itself as an economical alternative to the New York tourist or business traveler. It isn't quite as "sophisticated" as Holden describes it and probably never was. At 144 East 40th Street, just a couple of blocks from Grand Central Terminal, the uninspired brick facade is both uninviting and unprepossessing but the hotel itself offers clean, attractive rooms both with, and without, private bath. The *Seton Hotel* has no *Wicker Bar*; in fact, it has no bar at all.

Page 137: "Radio City...The Rockettes"

(See **Chapter 10,** Page 105-106: **"Radio City Music Hall"**)

(See **Chapter 17,** Page 181-182: **"...ice skating at Radio City..."**)

Page 138: "Kettle drums"

Tympani. Like many percussionists, the tympani player spends more time waiting and counting than actually playing. Nevertheless, the tympani are very cool percussion instruments and the player is a "superstar".

Page 140: "...the best war poet..."

Though it is clear what point D.B. is trying to make his example is odd and, to some degree, inept. To begin with Emily Dickinson (1830-1886), though she did write many of her poetic works during the American Civil War, has never been classified as a "war poet". She did write poems on the horrors and tragedies of America's most devastating conflict but – since she almost never left home - from the point of view of an observer. Her thoughts about and

Emily Dickinson

reactions to war were necessarily cerebral and philosophical.

Rupert Brooke (1887-1915) is most certainly considered a war poet, but his popularity with the British reading public had more to do with his youthful good looks and patriotism than his insights into martial conflict. In addition, Brooke had the good fortune to die young - always an invaluable aid to the legacy of a beautiful and talented young man. Septic pneumonia condemned him to a hasty Greek burial prior to what very likely would have been a violent death at Gallipoli. So, on the one hand you have a woman who rarely strayed from her family home, found comfort in a life of clock-work domesticity, and wrote occasionally of the grief and horror war inflicts upon mortals; and on the other a war casualty described by W.B. Yeats as "the handsomest young man in England" whose poems extolled the noble sacrifice of the patriotic combatant.

Rupert Brooke

Mark Twain wrote, "War talk by men who have been in a war is always interesting; whereas moon talk by a poet who has not been in the moon is likely to be dull". It might have been fairer of D.B. to compare the work of Brooke to that of Siegfried Loraine Sassoon (1886 –1967) who saw combat in the same war, survived, and wrote bitterly of war's folly, hypocrisy and foolishness.

Allie, after retrieving his baseball mitt, declares Emily Dickinson the better war poet – though what Allie's mitt has to do with the question isn't clear, unless it was wrapped around an anthology of martial verse. This is apparently the answer D.B. is looking for since he seems to have nothing more to say on the subject. Allie's response supports D.B.'s tacit assertion that one does not need to experience war to know its awful truths. Whether or not you agree with D.B. and Allie, the argument used in reaching that conclusion is twisted.

Page 140: "...he landed on D-Day and all..."

On June 6, 1944, J.D. Salinger, along with thousands of other young Americans, boarded an amphibious troop carrier and crossed the English Channel to the thundering chaos of Normandy's beaches. Like all the rest he stepped out into cold seawater and the threat of violent death; like many of the fortunate ones he made it to the beach, dug in and began firing on German artillery emplacements. At the conclusion of D-Day Salinger's regiment had progressed nearly two miles inland toward Cherbourg. Other than the mundane itinerary of time and place, little is known of Salinger's thoughts about his years of service in Europe during W.W. II.

Given Holden's youth it was necessary for Salinger to transfer his wartime service to D.B.

Page 141: "A Farewell to Arms"

The J.D. Salinger/Ernest Hemingway (1899-1961) connection makes for an interesting, if short, story. By the time Salinger went to war he had read all of Ernest Hemingway's short stories and novels published to that point. In fact, by 1940 Hemingway's best work was behind him. From then until his death in 1961 only a handful of short stories, *A Moveable Feast* and *The Old Man and the Sea* count as substantial contributions to his literary legacy. A fortuitous encounter at the *Ritz Hotel* in 1944 marked the only time the two writers would meet face to face. Salinger was suitably in awe of his older mentor and Hemingway, no doubt flattered, was encouraging and helpful to the younger aspiring writer who had already had work published in *Story* magazine and the *Saturday Evening Post*. Salinger's youth and obsequiousness no doubt elicited the kind of indulgence Hemingway reserved for fawning young males and pretty girls. He was notoriously competitive and had already acquired a reputation for turning on his friends and ridiculing the work of literary peers. (Gore Vidal "detest(ed) him" and thought him a poseur, John Steinbeck found him "incredibly vain" and Truman Capote called him "a mean man".)

In a letter from J.D. Salinger stationed in Occupied Germany to Ernest Hemingway in the summer of 1946 he says that he is working on a play about a character named Holden Caulfield. His tone is light and friendly and at one point fancifully suggests that in a dramatic version of what would eventually become *The*

Margaret O'Brien

Catcher in the Rye he should play the part of Holden Caulfield and MGM contract-ingénue Margaret O'Brien play Phoebe. He curiously referred to his Holden/Phoebe stories as "incestuous" and had all but given up plans for a novel. Salinger was very careful to remind Hemingway that their meeting at the Ritz in 1944 had provided him with his only "moments of hopefulness" during the war and declared himself Chairman of the "Hemingway Fan Clubs".

Hemingway read *The Catcher in the Rye* when it was published in 1951. His copy remains in the library of his Cuba home, La Finca Vigia. No doubt he would have been put off by Holden's criticisms of *A Farewell to Arms* and the reference to Lt Henry as a "phony". Hemingway was known to have been thrown into rages by far less critical comments. Yet he may also have recognized it as akin to what he himself had done when he cruelly parodied his own mentor, Sherwood Anderson, in *Torrents of Spring* twenty-five years earlier.

After 1951 there is no record of communication between the two writers. However, in March of 1952, already in literary decline and fearing the loss of his creative fires, Hemingway returned to his earlier territory of Michigan and wrote one more of his Nick Adams stories in which the young man's relationship with his younger sister, Littless, has been termed "quasi-incestuous" and apparently influenced by his reading of Salinger's novel the previous year.

Depressed and in ill health, Hemingway committed suicide in 1961.

Page 141: "The Great Gatsby"

F. Scott Fitzgerald's 1925 masterpiece is considered by many to be the perfect, if not "Great", American novel. Though disappointingly unsuccessful on publication, it was rediscovered in the 1950's and acclaimed as an American classic. Both Holden and his creator, J.D. Salinger, admired the novel.

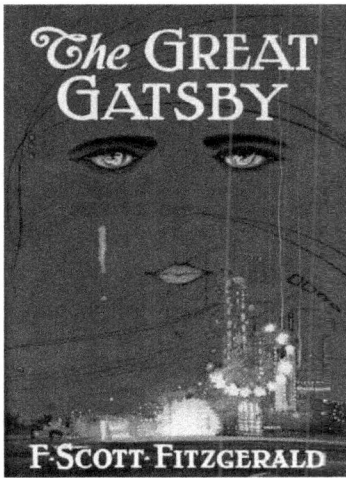

The only significant connections between *The Great Gatsby* and *The Catcher in the Rye* are that both titles refer to the main character and first-person narrators tell both stories.

Page 141: "I'm going to sit right the hell on top of (the atomic bomb)."

Following World War II the all-consuming fear of Atomic weapons haunted Americans of all political persuasions. Everyone knew that the Soviet Union had acquired Atomic weapons and fearfully anticipated the day they might decide to drop what became colloquially known as "the bomb". There is no modern equivalent except perhaps the generalized fear of terrorist acts following the September 11th attack on New York's World Trade Center in 2001.

Holden's comment may have inspired the scene in Stanley Kubrick's 1964 film classic *Dr. Strangelove, or: How I Learned to Stop Worrying and Love the bomb* where Major "King" Kong (played by character actor Slim Pickens) rides an Atomic bomb

out of its bay like a rodeo rider astride a bucking bronco.

Chapter 19

(Sunday, early evening)

In which Holden meets Luce for a drink at the Wicker Bar.

> Hearts seem light, and life seems bright,
> In dreamy Chinatown!
> > William Jerome and Jean Schwartz, 1910

> They hug and kiss each night,
> By jingo, boys, worth that price!
> Back in Nagasaki
> Where the fellows chew tobaccky
> And the women wicky-wacky-woo!
> > Harry Warren and Mort Dixon, 1928

Page 141: "Seton Hotel"

(See Chapter 17, **Page 137: "Wicker Bar on 54th"**)

Page 142: "louse"

A "louse" is a term used to describe a perfectly awful person; a cruel or thoughtless individual; someone to be avoided at all costs.

A true louse is a wingless, parasitic insect. As an order (Phthiraptera) there are more than 3,000 species. Lice lay their eggs in their host's hair. Designed for tenacity (as opposed to speed or cunning), they spend their entire lives on one creature.

Unlike human "louses"[58], insect lice vary little in appearance, however features shared by both varieties are their unpleasantness and the difficulties one much endure to be rid of them.

Page 142: "full of flits"

Flits are gay men. The slang goes back at least to the end of the nineteenth century. It is thought that this usage derives from one of the original meanings of the word *flit*: to fly lightly from place to place; to flutter. Since the 1890's male homosexuals have been referred to as "fairies"; fairies flutter from place to place, ergo the verb *to flit* becomes the noun *flit*. (Some hold that "FLIT" is an acronym, but I don't buy that for a minute.)

---

[58] The plural of "louse" is "lice", providing it is an insect. In humans a collection of more than one louse is properly referred to as "louses"… or a "frat-boys".

Of course real fairies prefer gossamer gowns to tattersall vests, but Holden could hardly be expected to have learned that from reading *Beowulf.*

In the 1940's and 50's FLIT was a well-known brand of insecticide used to combat mosquitoes in domestic and commercial environments. Theodor Geisel – years before he

became world-famous as Dr. Seuss -created the artwork for a long-running series of ads that made "Quick, Henry, the FLIT!" one the most popular catchphrases of the Eisenhower era.

Page 143: "Old Luce"

Luce is not particularly old. The term "old" often implies *of long standing* when put before a noun; i.e. "old friend", "old buddy", "old girl", etc. For Holden to use the term "Old Luce" when referring to his friend suggests an intimacy or long-term friendship that might be another of Holden's exaggerations.

Holden's "Old Luce" is reminiscent of Jay Gatsby's use of "old sport" when addressing friends and associates in *The Great Gatsby*.

Page 143: "Joe Blow"

Mr. Joe Blow is a typical guy; your average person; any anonymous individual.

Joe has, since the early 1900's, been the name of choice for a generic male; before that it was John, Tom or Dick. Joe's last name has been variously given as *Zilch*, *Shmo*, or *Blow* . In American Yiddish a *shmo* is a foolish or stupid person.

(See Chapter 12, Page 117: **"Joe-Yale looking-guy"**, also Chapter 14, Page 133: **"Holy Joe"**)

Page 143: "...you could turn into one practically overnight..."

One of the persistent myths surrounding homosexuality is that it is contagious or a sort of acquired taste to which one becomes habituated over time. The idea that one could turn gay from exposure to homosexual men, or catch "gayness" through air-borne transmission wasn't completely debunked until the beginning of the twenty-first century. Even so, some remain unconvinced and the myth presists.

Page 144: "Columbia"

Founded by George II, Kings College, now Columbia University, is a private university in New York City and the oldest institute of higher education in the state. Founded in

1754 it is one of the Ivy League colleges. It is located on thirty-two acres of prime real estate in the Morningside Heights neighborhood of Manhattan a few blocks north of Central Park and just off the Hudson River.

Page 145: "Nantucket"

Another joke; if not Holden's, then Salinger's. Nantucket, Massachusetts is a small island south of Cape Cod. At one time it was the most important whaling port in the world. Now its primary economic value is as a tourist destination and home to the very wealthy. However, by far the most noteworthy thing about Nantucket is its prominence in a well-known obscene limerick.

A limerick is a five-line poem of inflexible meter instantly recognized by pub-crawlers, frat boys and grade school children in all English speaking countries. If a technical definition is required, here it is: Of the five lines in a limerick lines one, two and five consist of three anapestic feet, while the third and fourth lines have two feet each. The rhyme scheme is *aabba*. Any decent limerick must either be clever, humorous or obscene. A combination of any two of those - or, saints be praised, all three - raises the effort to that of divine writ.

For example:

> *There was a young lady of Lynn,*
> *Who was so excessively thin.*
> *That when she assayed*
> *To drink lemonade,*
> *She slipped through the straw and fell in.*

Or

> *A hit-man from Washington state*
> *Whose girth was alarmingly great*
> *Knew his fondness for killing*
> *Meant no one was willing*
> *To tell him he ought to lose weight.*

The limerick in question begins, "There was a young man from Nantucket..." and from there descends immediately into an appallingly graphic depiction of autoeroticism carried to wondrous extremes. If you want to read the complete work you can find it on-line. While the verse exists in multiple versions and permutations the differences are relatively minor and the essential depravity remains the same throughout. The author of this lyric has wisely chosen to remain anonymous; it is thought to date from the early twentieth century.

Page 146: "...martini...a lot dryer"

Ask someone to name a cocktail and they'll probably answer, "martini". It is the archetypical cocktail which H.L. Mencken declared "the only American invention as perfect as the sonnet". The favorite quote of martini lovers everywhere, "Let's get out of these wet clothes and into a dry martini" has been attributed to such personalities as Billy Wilder, Robert Benchley, Mae West, Grouch Marx and Alexander Woolcot. (Benchley gets the most votes.)

The origins of the martini are obscure and its premier, depending on whose word you take, may have been either Oslo, San Francisco or New York. A simple drink to make, all one need do is combine five parts gin to one part dry vermouth in a mixing glass with ice. Stir or shake these ingredients, pour into a cocktail glass and add either an olive or a twist of lemon peel. Wham; that's it.

As one might expect with so simple a procedure real martini aficionados have evolved all kinds of rituals, accessories and superstitions to accompany their favorite buzz. The obsession with *dryness* is widespread. The vermouth must be very dry; the quantity of vermouth must be reduced to the point where it becomes almost homeopathic; only a particular brand of vermouth is acceptable, etc. Or you can fret over how the ingredients are mixed; James Bond, as we all know, wanted his "shaken, not stirred". Some prefer a martini made with vodka instead of gin; others argue that unless it is gin-based it isn't a real martini at all and has to have another name like "vodka-tini". A martini with an olive or a lemon twist is still a martini, but if you put in an olive the cocktail becomes a "Gibson". The old story goes that if you are ever hopelessly lost in the arctic all you need do is begin to prepare a martini and someone will immediately turn up to show you how you are doing it wrong.

Page 146: "You mean its better in China?"

Since at least 1848 when Commodore Peary opened Japan to

the western world men, and American men in particular, have had a peculiar fascination with Asian women. A whole mythology has been created around their extraordinary sexual powers, talents and practices that has no doubt come as a surprise to Asian men. How this all got started is not clear. Most likely the first American sailors and soldiers stationed in the far east came home with stories – true or apocryphal - to rival those of their states-bound brethren. In the same way that American doughboys popularized fabulous tales of French erotomania, American sailors and G.I.'s came home from Hawaii, the Philippines, China and the South Seas with tales to rival those of Marco Polo or the Baron Munchhausen. And it wasn't always a question of attitudes, technique or expertise; Asian women were actually credited with physiological differences enabling them to draw their lovers to the absolute limits of sexual pleasure.

Page 148: "psychoanalyst"

A social phenomenon peculiar to Americans in the first half of the twentieth century was a fear and suspicion of psychiatry. Many social historians link this distrust to the Freudian[59] emphasis on sexuality as the source and repository of childhood and infant trauma. Americans have never been comfortable with discussions of sexual matters and the mere suggestion of childhood sexuality was enough to throw U.S. men and women into a frenzy of denial. In films of the 30's and 40's the

Sigmund Freud

psychiatrist or psychologist is depicted as a nut bent on perverting or destroying our most cherished values, beliefs and fantasies.

In *The Catcher in the Rye* this is probably not the case, since the entire novel is framed by Holden's telling of his story to a doctor of psychology or psychiatry – a very patient one, I might add. But having a character like Luce, a self-important, neurasthenic, pseudo-intellectual of ambiguous sexuality, proclaim that his father is a psychiatrist suggests an uncomfortable philosophical duality on the part of the author.

Page 148: "I have to tear..."

---

[59] Named for Sigmund Freud (pronounced 'froid'), the so-called 'father of modern psychiatry'.

That is, "I have to leave quickly". Similar to the more contemporary, "Gotta split", "I'm outta here", or "Ya me voy".

Chapter 20

(Sunday evening)

In which Holden makes a drunken phone call to Sally, visits the frozen pond in Central park and thinks dark thoughts.

> Me and my shadow,
> Strolling down the avenue,
> Me and my shadow,
> Not a soul to tell our troubles to...
> > Billy Rose, 1927

Page 149: "I sort of gave her the old eye..."

To *give someone the eye* is to visually inspect or attempt communication solely by means of a glance, look, wink or squint. The expression is almost always used in a romantic or sexual way. When the look isn't amatory the expression is altered slightly to *wry eye*, *evil eye*, *stink eye*, etc.

Page 150: "...dial about twenty numbers..."

From its invention in 1886 to the mid-1960's nearly all telephones used a rotary dial to register numbers through to the switchboard or automated relay station. A round dial perforated with ten finger-sized holes was mounted on the front of the telephone console. Each hole corresponded to a number from 1 to "0" and either two or three letters of the alphabet - the number 1 had no letters associated with it. The letters were not used for sending text messages - that was impossible in those days - but for dialing prefixes. A prefix was a series of two letters (and, after 1950, a number) which preceded the four digit telephone number. Once the telephone had become so popular that all possible four-digit combinations had been used up, prefixes were necessary to separate telephone numbers by geographic area or *exchange*. Depending on where one lived, the prefix was a word exclusively assigned to that *exchange*, i.e, CIrcle, ENdicott, PLaza, MAdison, ELdorado (all common Manhattan prefixes).

Only the first two letters were dialed regardless of how many letters were in the prefix word. In the late 1940's a digit was added to each exchange (EXeter-5, for example)[60] so Holden never needed to dial more than two letters and five digits to give anyone in New York a "buzz".

The person making the call would insert a finger into the desired number or letter and pull the dial in a clockwise direction. When released the dial would automatically return to its former position and a series of rapid clicks was heard on the receiver. These clicks were the audible *pulses* that gave *pulse*

---

[60] In the 50's Lucy and Ricky Ricardo could have been "buzzed" at either Murray Hill 5-9975, Circle 7-2099, or Murray Hill 5-9099

dialing its name. The dialer would repeat this procedure through all six (or seven) letters and digits. Anything more complicated than that, long-distance for example, required the services of a telephone operator. Repeated dialing could give one pain in the index finger, so plastic dialing tools became popular with salesmen and secretaries.

In the 1960's *touch-tone* dialing began to replace *pulse* dialing and telephones were equipped with a pad of 12 buttons instead of a dial - though the process of registering numbers was still, paradoxically, called "dialing". The "1" button still had no letters of the alphabet associated with it, "O" was labeled "OPER" for operator, and the "star" and "pound" keys were added (to the confusion of many since it was decades before they had any practical purpose).

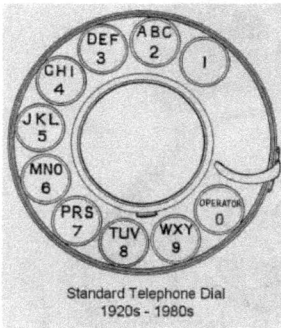

Standard Telephone Dial
1920s - 1980s

The quaint prefix names we'd all grown used to were ultimately phased out in favor of numerical designations. Exeter-5, for example, became simply 395.

Page 150: "Attaboy"

This is a common exclamation of encouragement and approval shortened from "That's my boy!"

Page 151: "Rocky's"

Holden is not referring to any particular Rocky, but simply using it as a label for an all-purpose tough guy.

Americans love gangster movies. From the rise of the mob in the 1920's through prohibition, Warner Brothers Studios in Burbank, California alone cranked out dozens of them. At least in part because Warner's had access to so many of the great tough guys (Humphrey Bogart, James Cagney, George Raft and Edward G. Robinson) these films became, for a while, the house specialty. Gangsters sometimes had names from the headlines like Clyde, John, George or Alphonse, but preferred tough-sounding monikers like Rico, Tony, "Gat" or, why not, Rocky.

In the 1938 Warner Bros. Film, *Angels with Dirty Faces*, James Cagney played the role of tough-guy Rocky Sullivan. Rocky and Hugo were the gangster supporting players to Bugs Bunny in the 1946 Warner Bros. cartoon "Racketeer Rabbit"[61]. Later, Rocky and a new side-kick, Mugsy were paired in several Warner cartoons made between 1950 and 1963.[62]

Page 151: "Andover jerk"

Phillips Academy in Andover, Massachusetts (21 miles north of Boston) is another exclusive prep school – presumably one Holden has not attended. Founded in 1778 it is the nation's oldest prep school. George Washington spoke there in 1789. Philips Academy went coed in 1973 when it merged with Abbot Academy.

While there have been no formal studies, it is unlikely that Andover has any more jerks than any other school.

(See Chapter 17, Page 180: **"jerks"**)

Page 152: "radiator"

Before the invention of forced-air heating the most common way to effectively heat large buildings was with a central furnace that pumped steam through pipes to radiators installed in each room. The furnace, large and noisy, was generally located in

---

[61] It must be noted that in this cartoon the characters of Rocky and Hugo were modeled after Edward G. Robinson and Peter Lorre, respectively. See note above: page 103: **"Peter Lorre"**

[62] Rocky Balboa, Rocky Raccoon and Rocky (Rocket J.) Squirrel were to come along later.

the basement of the building, regularly stoked with coal or oil and maintained by a custodian or building superintendent through the winter months. An elaborate system of pipes and valves transported the steam to each radiator, a vertical assembly of iron pipes through which steam was pumped. The steam released its heat within the upper regions of the radiator then condensed to the lower sections where it was forced back down to the furnace for re-heating. Individual controls allowed the user to adjust room temperature by admitting more or less steam into the radiator. The system was temperamental and prone to malfunction. Tenants commonly complained of

getting too much or, more commonly, not enough heat. Expansion and contraction of metal conduits often caused loud banging sounds, and air trapped in the pipes interfered with the flow of heat.

Page 152: "Mac"

"Mac" is any male person whose name you do not know. Similar to "Buddy", "Pal" or, more recently, "Dude" it is an extremely informal – some would say impolite – form of address. The word derives from the *Mac* or *Mc* which precedes many Scottish surnames. Eventually whether one was talking to a MacDougal, a McCarthy, a MacGillicuddy or a Schwartz a simple "Mac" would suffice.

Page 152: "eighty-six"

Another joke. To "eighty-six" something or someone is to eject, reject or dismiss. As with most slang terms the origins of this phrase are in question, but it is widely believed to have been code-talk among waiters and bartenders. "Eighty-six" variously meant that some item on the menu was no longer available, that some customer needed to be shown the door, or that the person in question had already had more than enough to drink. If you were the one being eighty-six'ed your requests for service were ignored and/or you were asked to leave.

The highland fling

Page 152: "sack"

Bed.

Page 153: "started chattering like hell"

If your teeth chatter due to cold it's called *involuntary thermoregulation*. In an effort to create warmth small muscles automatically begin to contract resulting in teeth chattering, the tightening of hair follicles and generalized shivers. If you were to, say, put on a sweater, jump in a hot tub, do some push-ups or run around in circles your teeth would stop chattering.

However, what Holden is very likely experiencing is a *panic attack* or a symptom of an *anxiety disorder*. Symptoms of a *panic attack* can include: nausea, chills, shivering (and teeth-chattering), shortness of breath, the feeling that one's heart is pounding or racing, tingling or numbness in the hands, and heavy perspiration. Individuals who are experiencing a panic attack often fear that they will lose control, go crazy or die during the episode. In the final chapters of *The Catcher in the Rye,* Holden experiences many of these symptoms. Any confusion in diagnosing his problem arises from the fact that he is also undernourished, drunk, wet and very cold.

Page 154: "...I went in the park. Boy, was it dark."

American composer Charles Ives wrote *"Central Park in the Dark"* in 1906. Ives, an experimental composer, adopted a densely layered, impressionistic approach to suggest the auditory impressions of a visitor on a walking tour through the park in the evening. Along with ambient sounds and musical motifs to suggest the activities taking place in the urban refuge, Ives incorporates at least five popular songs into his score including, "Hello! Ma Baby!", "The Campbells are Comin'", and John Philip Sousa's "Washington Post March".

The work had its world premier in New York in 1946.

The very first recorded version was released in 1951, the same year as *The Catcher in the Rye's* publication.

Page 156: "...superintendent's a lazy bastard..."

All residential complexes had superintendents or "supers" to handle general maintenance and repairs. The superintendent was given free or discounted rent in exchange for his duties. Inefficiency and tardiness in response to urgent needs were common complaints of tenants.

Chapter 21

(Late Sunday night)

In which Holden steals home to see Phoebe.

> A garden inclosed is my sister, my spouse...
> *The Holy Bible*, Song of Solomon,
> King James Version (1611)

Page 157: "Dicksteins"

Another compound joke: The surname *Stein* is German for *stone* or *rock*. *Dick* is both a shortened version of *Richard* and a slang name for the penis. Get it? In addition, the name suggests a conscious homage to the genius English novelist Charles Dickens had for giving his characters humorous yet highly appropriate names.

Page 158: "...ears like a goddam bloodhound."

This is a weirdly mixed metaphor. Bloodhounds are noted for their keen sense of smell, not hearing; creatures that live in fear of being devoured by predators (like deer, rabbits, squirrels, Belgians) have exceptional auditory abilities. If Holden's mother had had floppy, furry ears that fell to her shoulders the remark might make more sense but would still be inaccurate given the intent of the comment.

Page 160: "Phoebe Weatherfield Caulfield, Esq."

In England the sons of wealthy landowners and noblemen who had no other claim to pretense would adopt *Esquire* as a title. No qualifications were necessary or required. Eventually it came to take the place of Mr. on documents and contracts. Technically, there are no female *Esquires,* though in America lawyers of either sex have been known to use the *Esq.* after their names.

Of course Holden notices that the middle name, *Weatherfield,* isn't correct either.

Page 161: "Whenja..."

A verbal corruption of *When did you...?*

Page 162: "Benedict Arnold"

As far as Americans are concerned the name Benedict Arnold is synonymous with trator, dirty rat, sneakin' sidewinder or back-stabbin' mo-fo. Arnold, originally on the fast-track to hero-hood, had been a general in the Continental Army with a reputation for strategic cunning and battlefield courage.

When he failed to receive the credit he felt he deserved for the campaigns at Fort Ticonderoga and Saratoga (where he had sustained serious injuries) he began contemplating a career move, sideways. General Arnold arranged with the British to hand over West Point, New York, to British General Henry Clinton for twenty thousand pounds sterling but when the plot was discovered Arnold fled to join the dark forces for the rest of what came to be called the American Revolutionary War. After Britain lost the war Arnold moved with his family to London where he was never quite as welcome as he had hoped.

Page 162: "The Doctor...Lister Foundation"

The reasons for the inclusion of Phoebe's anecdote are unclear. Obviously a story dealing with euthanasia and the death of a child should resonate with Holden and the idea of a dead child's ghost returning to thank the doctor for killing her is melodramatic and downright macabre, but Holden is so wrapped up in finding out when his parents will be returning that he isn't even paying attention.

Joseph Lister (1827 – 1912) was a pioneer in the belief that micro-organisms / germs spread disease. While working as a doctor in Scotland he instituted procedures, policies and the widespread use of carbolic acid to sterilize surgical areas and clean wounds in Glasgow hospitals. There is currently a Lister Foundation, but it is a separate humanitarian entity of Lister Technologies and unrelated to the one Phoebe refers to.

In Britain there is a Lister Institute, founded in 1891 for the purpose of promoting advances in preventive medicine. The annual prizes give young scientists the opportunity to develop their research careers by offering three years of flexible support.

It is also possible that Phoebe is referring to the activities of the Pasteur Institute, named for the French microbiologist Louis Pasteur (1822 – 1895) whose work is often linked with that of Lister. Pasteur's theories regarding germs assisted in developing attitudes about cleanliness that greatly reduced the deaths of

Louis Pasteur

mothers immediately following childbirth. He created the first anti-rabies vaccine. Pasteur and Lister, have both been memorialized as two of the most important early scientists waging battle against pernicious diseases: Pasteurization, the process by which milk, wine and other liquids are cleansed of pathogens, was named for one; Listerine, a popular mouthwash since the late 19th century, for the other. Operating out of its headquarters in Paris, the Pasteur Institute works to further the study of disease-causing bacteria and the worldwide use of vaccines.

Page 163: "We have a radio in it now!"

From 1927 to 1933 car owners could have portable, battery-powered "travel radios" installed in their cars for a king's ransom, but it was not until the mid-1930's that radios became available as a factory-installed option on new cars. Because of

No stereo, no FM, no bass control, no Bluetooth, no...

the Depression and the subsequent reduction in automobile manufacturing brought about by World War II steel shortages most people did not have radios in their cars until after 1945.

Page 163: "...nobody can play it when the car's in traffic."

In the modern era of multitasking when drivers commonly talk on cell phones, read, shave, maintain oral hygiene and eat, one might find it hard to believe that there was a time when listening to the radio was considered a dangerous distraction.

Page 163: "plastered"

Synonymous with "wasted", "well-oiled", "borracho", "blotto", "pie-eyed", "SWAKed", "smashed", "inebriated", "blitzed", etc.; Drunk.

Page 164: "Annapolis"

The United States Naval Academy in Annapolis, Maryland was founded by the Secretary of the Navy, George Bancroft, in 1845. The biggest single attraction in Annapolis, the naval Academy sits on 238 acres just 33 miles east of Washington,

D.C.. As one might expect of so august an institution, the admission process is rigorous and designed to weed-out all but the most highly qualified candidates. To receive an appointment to the Naval Academy one must obtain a nomination from a United States Representative, two Senators or the Vice President. Naval Academy graduates enter active service as officers. Notable graduates include President Jimmy Carter, billionaire and former presidential candidate H. Ross Perot, Senator John McCain, Fleet Admiral Chester W. Nimitz and astronaut Alan Shepard.

Chapter 22

(Late Sunday night)

In which Holden tells Phoebe of his plan to save children from falling over the edge.

> Life is a horizontal fall.
> Jean Cocteau, 1930

Page 167: "...bull session..."

A "bull session" is a meeting or discussion; often a sustained period of conversation during which at least some of what is said is known to be false. The "bull" is shortened from "bullshit" a slang term for lies, boasting or idle talk.

Page 170: "...laying right on the stone steps and all..."

While Salinger was attending Valley Forge Military Academy a student fell to his death from an upper story dorm window. Foul play was never suspected; officials and students assumed he had slipped while trying to travel from one room to another via the roof. It is not known whether Salinger witnessed the event, but he obviously remembered it.

Page 173: "...I have to catch everybody if they start to go over the cliff..."

There is more at stake here than simply a drop from a great height. Using the word *fall* to signify a transgression or moral failing has been common since the 13th century. *Adam's fall* is his failure to do God's will and subsequent exile from Eden.

This is the *original sin* that some protestant faiths believe taints all mankind from birth. At the top of the standard "horn book" from which most colonial era children learned to read was the couplet, "In Adams' fall / We sinned all". The phrase *"fall from grace"* is used to denote the consequent reduction in one's perceived worth as a result of a misdeed, error or moral failing.

Holden knows he is speaking metaphorically. His desire is to save children from more than just physical harm. Their souls are at stake; if not in any strictly religious sense, metaphysically nevertheless.

Chapter 23

In which Holden and Phoebe are interrupted by their mother, Phoebe offers her brother a large sum of money, and Holden leaves the apartment.

> Dance with me
> I want my arms about you
> Those charms about you
> Will carry me through...
> To heaven, I'm in heaven...
> Irving Berlin, 1935

Page 175: "...corny dips..."

A "dip" is a dance position in which the female[63], back arched, drives her hips toward the male with one leg extended while he provides support to her lower back with one hand. (It looks a whole lot less awkward than it sounds.) This lunge is called a *dip* in a waltz, and a *corte* in a tango.. A similar move in greco-roman wrestling is called a *mistake*.

---

[63] In the event of both partners being of the same sex, a coin might be flipped to determine who is the dipper and who the dippee.

Page 177: "Phoebe, have you been smoking...?"

Modern readers find Phoebe's mother's response to her daughter's smoking alarmingly inadequate and jump to erroneous conclusions about her maternal failings. It does need to be noted that attitudes toward smoking in the late 1940's were very different than they are today. In post W.W.II America smoking was regarded as an adult pastime in much the same way as coffee drinking is today. It was generally believed

that smoking could harm the lungs in some unspecified way, and children were admonished that it would "stunt (their) growth", but there was no widespread understanding of the harmful or addictive properties of tobacco. Cigarettes were freely advertised on radio and- when it came into homes in the late forties - television. Cigarette consumption was promoted with outlandishly false claims and promises. At once cool, manly, feminine, sophisticated, relaxed, aggressive, stylish, fun and thoughtful, cigarettes were advertised as "safe" and came with a physician's seal of approval. Candy cigarettes[64] were a very popular treat with the kiddies. While outwardly discouraging cigarette smoking, adults at least tacitly knew their children would end up smoking sooner or later and usually overlooked, if not condoned, youthful experimentation. The fact is, given the time and place Mrs. Caulfield may well have had more important things to worry about than whether or not Phoebe experimented with a very common adult behavior.

Page 180: "garbage pails"

In the 1940's mechanical garbage disposals were illegal in New York City. In fact, mechanical garbage disposals were prohibited in Manhattan until 1997 because of the primitive nature of the century-old underground sewage system that did not separate waste-water from raw sewage. All residents of Manhattan collected their garbage in small kitchen containers and galvanized steel pails that were left out for periodic collection by city-contracted waste disposal vehicles - often mob-owned.

Though invented in the late 1920's, very few American homes had mechanical waste disposal units in their kitchens in the 1940's and 50's.

---

[64] Most commonly these were made of chocolate wrapped in thin paper or rolled from a brittle, chalky-white substance with the "lit" end stained red.

Chapter 24

(The "wee hours",[65] Monday morning)

In which Holden goes to visit the Antolini's, is offered advice and a place to sleep, and is frightened away.

> If you ever lose your mind, I'll be kind.
> And if you ever lose your shirt, I'll be hurt.
> If you're ever in a mill and get sawed in half, I won't laugh.
> It's friendship....
> Cole Porter, 1939

Page 180: "Sutton Place"

Today this is a very exclusive neighborhood with expensive lofts, townhomes and condominiums overlooking the East River. Between 53rd Street and the Queensboro Bridge, Sutton Place runs north from just above the United Nations building to 60th Street where it becomes York Ave. The Antolini's would not have lived very far from Holden's parents' apartment on 71st Street east of the park.[66]

---

[65] The "wee hours" refers to the single digits just after midnight; one o'clock, two o'clock, etc. I don't know how far one can go and still be in the "wee hours", but I suppose it would be fair to say that four o'clock is the limit. Certainly five o'clock is two late to be "wee".

[66] About the same time as this story is being told, new residents in the neighborhood would include the Ricardos (Lucy and Ricky) and the Mertzes (Fred and Ethel) at 628 E. 68th Street. (That E. 68th Street goes no further than the 500 block before encountering the East River seemed to pose no problem to any of them.)

Page 180/181: "West Side Tennis Club, in Forest Hills, Long Island"

(See Chapter 15, page 151: "Nationals at Forest Hills")

Page 181: " a highball..."

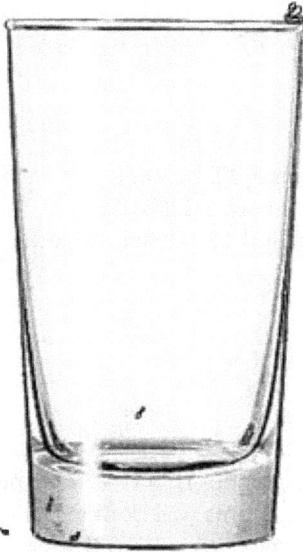

A highball is a tall slender glass with a capacity of 8 to 12 ounces used for serving light spirits and mixed drinks like a White Russian, Tequila Sunrise or Long Island Iced Tea. Sometimes the word "*highball*" is used to imply any mixed drink.

Page 181: "...day-old infant in your arms. Nowhere to turn."

Mr. Antolini is facetiously alluding to the literary cliche in which the wayward daughter, having left home against her parent's wishes and embarked on an ill-considered life with an unreliable young man, returns, chastened, humbled and contrite to the home she had so unwisely abandoned. (Add snowflakes for additional pathos.) Tess Durbeyfield finds herself in a similar predicament in Thomas Hardy's *Tess of the d'Urbervilles: A Pure Woman Faithfully Presented (1891)*. A stock element of Victorian era plotting and stage melodrama of the mid-19th century, the "prodigal daughter returned" became a device as corny as the mustached villain who twirls his mustache and laughs "Nyah - ah - ah!" while tying virgins to the railroad tracks.

Page 182: "oiled up"

Inebriated, drunk, intoxicated, plastered...

Page 182: "...Buffalo friends...some buffaloes..."

A lame joke equating friends from the city of Buffalo, New York with the North American Bison (commonly called a "buffalo"). You'd have to be pretty "oiled up" to find it funny.

Page 183: "Richard Kinsella"

A contemporary coincidence: The author W(illiam) P(atrick) *Kinsella* wrote *Shoeless Joe,* a novel that was later made into the movie *Field of Dreams* starring Kevin Costner . In the novel the protagonist, Ray Kinsella, seeks out J.D. Salinger (reclusive author Terrence Mann in the film version) in order to help him understand his connection with the disgraced baseball player Shoeless Joe Jackson and, in turn, his own father. The fictional Salinger regains his love of the national pastime.

Professionally, both authors, Kinsella and Salinger, use only their first two initials. Kinsella was 19 when *The Catcher in the Rye* was published.

Page 184: "polio"

It's hard for modern readers to adequately appreciate the fear that polio (infantile paralysis) generated in the 1940's and 50's. The post-war epidemic resulted in 20,000 new cases each year from 1945-49. Nationwide, pediatric hospitals were filled with children whose paralysis had advance to the point where they could not

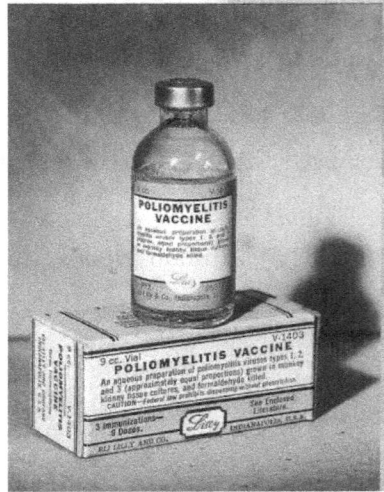

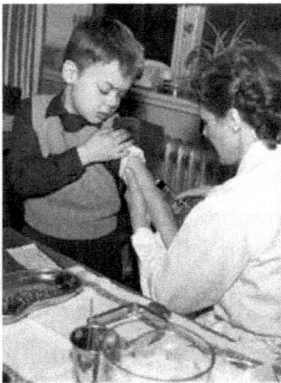

breathe on their own and had to be confined to cylindrical steel artificial respirators. Nearly every family in the country knew a friend or neighbor whose child had been stricken, never to walk again. At the time it was not clear how the virus was spread – though later it was learned that contaminated water was often the culprit - or why some people were susceptible while others were not.

Adults were not immune, Franklin Delano Roosevelt, the only U.S. president to have been so disabled, contracted polio in 1921. During the war the high incidence of polio among servicemen stationed in Africa, the Middle East and the Philippines confirmed the suspected role of primitive sanitation systems in the transmission of the virus.

First identified in 1908, the virus that caused entered the body orally, passed from the intestinal lining to the blood stream and, finally, attacked the central nervous system. The result was muscle weakness and, in many cases, paralysis.

By 1952 a vaccine devised by Jonas Salk was available for widespread use in this country, but it was not until 1957 that there was sufficient vaccine to reasonably protect the entire population. The combination of the Salk vaccine and the oral vaccine developed by Albert Sabin that largely replaced it in 1962 reduced the occurrence of the disease to 121 cases nationwide by 1964. In the mid-1990's it was thought that polio had been defeated worldwide, but outbreaks in Haiti and the Dominican Republic demonstrated the need for continued vigilance and distribution of vaccine.

In 2000 the new target date for global elimination of polio was set for 2005.

Currently (as of 2019), endemic transmission has continued in Afghanistan, Nigeria and Pakistan.

Page 185: "They were always kissing each other a lot in public."

Though we know very little about Mr. And Mrs. Antolini, there is reason to suspect that they lived what was called in the 1930's and 40's a "white marriage". In a "white marriage" – from the French *mariage blanc* - a gay man weds a woman – sometimes a lesbian woman – out of social expedience. The arrangement offered companionship, social acceptance and protection from rumors which might damage one's professional standing. Such arrangement were more common among gay men than lesbian women; it would seem that lesbians in general had less need of social camouflage. In the world of show business and politics such marriages of convenience were relatively common. There is a long list of contemporary partnerships in which one or both participants have been rumored or known to be gay: Cole Porter and divorcee Linda Thomas; former California Congressman Michael Huffington and writer Adrianna

Huffington; Rock Hudson and Phyllis Gates; Barbara Stanwyck and Robert Taylor; Judy Garland and Vincente Minnelli; their daughter, Lisa Minnelli married Australian singer/songwriter Peter Allen.

Page 186: "stenographer"

A *stenographer* is what would today be termed a secretary. Stenography - from the Greek *stenos* (tight, narrow) and *graphy* (writing) - was a general term for any of a variety of styles of shorthand transcription.

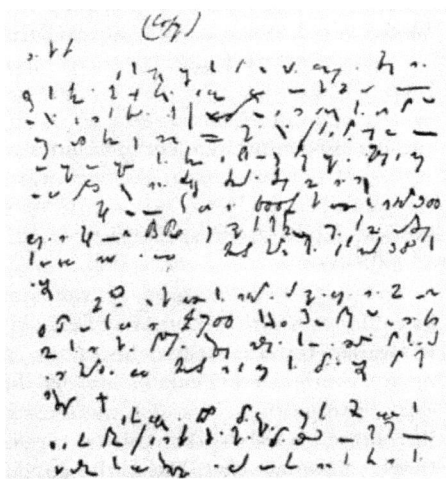

Charles Dickens practiced his shorthand in the London Courts of Law

From ancient times people who have had the desire to record thoughts, ideas and speeches quickly have developed methods for doing so. Since the 16th century such writers have either invented their own methods or learned systems by such inventors as Timothy Bright, John Willis, Isaac Pitman, Benn Pitman and Robert Gregg. (Two others I will include only because of their wonderful names are Hamden Forkner and Franz Xavier Gabelsberger.) Most of these systems look to the uninitiated like a series of squiggles or loosely-spaced Arabic. Gregg's system, introduced in 1888, became the standard for journalists and stenographers in the United States.

Fluency in shorthand transcription was a requirement for anyone seeking a secretarial position. Until the 1950's a course

236

in Gregg Shorthand was a required subject for girls in many American high schools. The invention of wire recorders, dictation machines and finally tape recorders marginalized the skill of stenography to the point where today few modern secretaries have ever seen it in practice, much less know how to use it.

Notable shorthand experts have included Elizabethan diarist Samuel Pepys, Victorian novelist Charles Dickens, American journalists H.L. Mencken , Ring Lardner and British playwright Joe Orton.

Page 187: "...this fall I think you're riding for..."

The metaphorical expression 'riding for a fall" calls on equestrian terminology to mean "headed for trouble". However much he's had to drink, Mr. Antolini is remarkably prescient in his analysis of Holden's crises. The reader may

 wonder at this point whether Antolini is basing his comments on observations made prior to Allie's death or if he is simply responding to changes he's noticed since that tragedy. Perhaps Mr. Antolini sees something of himself in Holden and is equating Holden's future with his own past. Either way he's right on target. Still, given his sensitivity to Holden's problems one also wonders why he thought it would be OK to sit in the dark "petting...or patting" Holden's head. And what "highly unworthy cause" does he think Holden is dying nobly for?

(See **Chapter 22; Page 229: "...I have to catch everybody if they start to go over the cliff...")**

Page 188: "...psychoanalyst named Wilhelm Stekel..."

Stekel, a Pole, was a follower of Freud until he and Alfred Adler broke away to found the *Zentralblatt für Psychoanalyse* . Stekel always had trouble maintaining relationships and was known to have been antagonistic to even his closest friends, of whom, as one might expect, he had few. Fleeing Hitler's Germany in the late 1930's neither improved his outlook nor saved his life. He committed suicide in 1940. The quote attributed to him in chapter 24 of *The Catcher in the Rye* is genuine. Appropriately he also wrote, "In reality, we are all still children. We want to find a playmate for our thoughts and feelings."

Page 193: "That kind of stuff's happened to me about twenty times..."

Even though Holden is do doubt exaggerating one might fairly wonder what reasons there could be for all of this "unwanted" homosexual attention. You don't have to be a licensed psychologist to question whether Holden is sending mixed signals.

Chapter 25

(Early Monday morning, December 19, 1949)

In which Holden goes looking for Phoebe at her school, is upset by what he finds there, returns to the park, is joined by Phoebe dragging a suitcase, and takes her to ride on the carousel.

> In the same hour came forth fingers of a man's hand, and wrote over against the candlestick upon the plaister of the wall...Then the king's countenance was changed, and his thoughts troubled him, so that the joints of his loins were loosed, and his knees smote one against another. This is the interpretation of the thing: ... Thou art weighed in the balances, and art found wanting.
>
> Book of Daniel 5: 1-27,
> King James Version, *The Holy Bible* (1611)

Page 194: "...I walked over to Lexington..."

Lexington is four long blocks west of Sutton Place. From there it is another ten to twelve short blocks to Grand Central Terminal.

Page 195: "hormones"

Hormones are the chemical means by which cells communicate. Produced by nearly every organ system in the body, hormones are released directly in to the blood stream, body fluids or adjacent tissues. Hormones regulate such processes as growth, cell mortality, metabolism, reproduction and the activation of the immune system. Holden does not need to worry about having "lousy" hormones; the important question is simply how well their production is regulated and whether they are present in the body in sufficient quantities when they are needed.

The first understanding of the function of hormones occurred in 1902 with the discovery of secretin by Ernest Starling. He did not use the term hormone until 1905.

The four types of human hormones are Lipid, Peptoid, Amine and Steroid. The most fascinating Lipid hormones are the prostaglandins. Peptoid hormones include growth hormone, secretin and insulin. Among the Amine hormones are serotonin, thyroxine, adrenaline and dopamine. The last of these groups contains cortisol and the sex steroids testosterone and progesterone. This is the group that Holden is concerned about and, when administered improperly, can bring about the dramatic physical and psychological changes so carefully scrutinized by athletic officials.

Page 197: "...un-loading this big Christmas tree off a truck..."

This passage was perhaps inspired by a similar scene in Betty Smith's *A Tree Grows in Brooklyn* (1943) where young Francie Nolan and her baby brother compete with other equally deprived neighborhood kids to catch leftover Christmas trees as they are chucked from the back end of a truck by two profane, and reluctant, working-class philanthropists.

Francie and her brother are bowled over and bruised by the flying evergreen, but together they drag it triumphantly home on Christmas Eve.

Holden would have loved Francie who, in many ways, seems a Phoebe prototype. The novel was hugely successful when Salinger was in his early twenties and seeing his stories first published in *The Saturday Evening Post* and *Story* magazine.

Page 197: "...Salvation Army girls..."

A common fantasy held that the women members of the

Salvation Army were only barely-reformed "women of the streets" and that with a little effort a motivated fellow might peel off that dark blue veneer of uniformed propriety and find a "tigress" longing to express her sublimated sexuality. In Frank Loesser's 1955 musical *"Guys and Dolls"*, Sister Sarah Brown of the *Save a Soul Mission* is targeted for such liberation by legendary gambler Sky Masterson.

(See **Chapter 15, Page 109: "Salvation Army...Christmas time..."**)

Page 197: "Bloomingdale's"

The flagship of this upscale department store chain is the one on 59th Street and Third Avenue. Founded in the 1860's by brothers Joseph and Lyman Bloomingdale, the two dealers in "European fashion" virtually invented the idea of the urban department store when, in 1886, they moved what had been the *East Side Bazaar* to its current address and changed the name.

Innovative marketing concepts and a generous advertising budget created a very successful brand-consciousness, and by the 1920 Bloomingdales filled an entire city block. A costly remodeling of the store resulted in the current Art Deco landmark with entrances on 59th and Lexington. New York's second most popular tourist attraction – just behind the Statue of Liberty – the legendary display windows have often been an attraction unto themselves. It wasn't until the late 1950's and

Bloomingdales downtown Manhattan store.

Bloomingdales opened a store outside of New York.

Bloomingdale's – "Bloomies" to Manhattanites - is now owned by Federated Department Stores which also owns the Macy's chain.

One more old joke:

> On her deathbed an elderly woman issues a final request that she be cremated and her ashes sprinkled over Bloomingdales.
>
> "But why," asks the attending minister.

"At least that way," gasps the old lady, "I know my sisters will visit me twice a week".

Page 197: "...and charged them..."

The idea of buying on credit is at least as old as pockets. Customarily shopkeepers kept records of purchases for all of

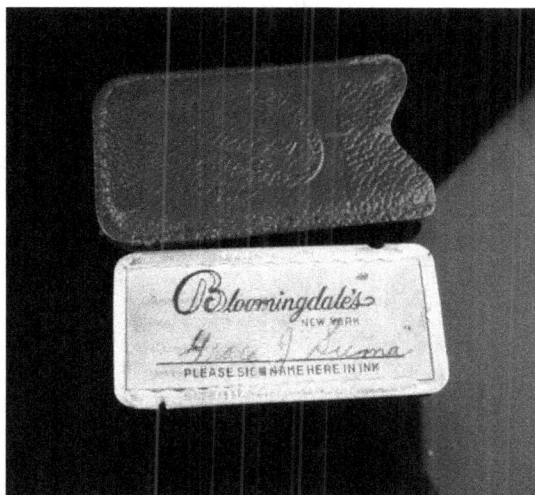

the regular customers and accounts were settled on payday. With the sudden popularity of automobiles in the 1920's gas companies started issuing "credit cards", often of stiff paper with an embossed metallic strip of numerals attached. "Charge plates" were commonly issued by individual merchants in the 1940's, but these were often kept at the establishment and useless in any other store. Bills were mailed to customers. This is the system Holden and Phoebe exploited at Bloomingdales.

In 1950 *Diner's Club*, followed shortly by *American Express*, issued the first real credit cards. As the names suggest, these cards were aimed primarily at businessmen (yeah, they were virtually all men) who traveled frequently and entertained clients in restaurants and hotel dining rooms. Balances were not carried over and users were expected to pay each month's bill in full. In 1958 Bank of America – formerly Bank of Italy

– issued the *BankAmericard*, the first credit card aimed at the general consumer. The *BankAmericard* became *Visa* in 1976. *Mastercharge*, which eventually became *Mastercard*, debuted in 1966.

Page 198: "...don't let me disappear."

Holden's fear of being swallowed up by the earth – another example of a fatal "fall" in this novel – is a manifestation of Holden's accelerating panic attacks.

(See **Chapter 20, Page 219: "...started chattering like hell..."**)

Page 198: "...up in the Sixties, past the zoo..."

Holden is sitting between "Kids Rock", a natural stone outcropping popular with local grade-schoolers, and the bronze statue of Balto, which has also been a favorite of children since its unveiling in 1925.

The real Balto, now stuffed, in the Cleveland Museum of Natural

Earlier that year Balto was the lead dog in a team that was credited with saving the lives of over three hundred people who had contracted diphtheria. After a blizzard had cut off train access to the isolated town of Nome, Alaska, twenty teams of over 200 dogs set out across a 667 mile segment of the Iditerod mail route between Nehana and Nome with diphtheria anti-toxin from Anchorage. People all over the country anxiously followed the story of the teams' progress over frigid, ice-bound tundra via newspaper and radio reports. Finally, after an astounding five days and seven hours of dog-sledding across a beak, frozen landscape, word went out that Gunnar Kasson had reached Nome with the life-saving serum in time to save the lives of the stricken townspeople. He and his steadfast team led by a black and white Alaskan malamute called Balto became instant celebrities. Balto's statue is located on top of a stone outcropping near the Willowdell Arch. Below Balto are inscribed the words, "Endurance, Fidelity, Intelligence".

Not far from Balto's statue and closer to Fifth Avenue is the memorial to the 107th Infantry (1926-27). The larger than life-size memorial depicts seven American soldiers in a tribute to the fallen of World War I. Sculptor Karl Illaya had been a sergeant in the 107th.

Page 198: "...Holland tunnel..."

Drivers entering Manhattan from New Jersey can do so via the *Holland tunnel* which enters the city at Spring Street near Soho. The *Lincoln Tunnel* and the *George Washington Bridge* are the other two ways of driving in from New Jersey.

Page 200: "...a colored kid .."

This marks the only appearance of a racial or ethnic minority in *The Catcher in the Rye*. (The Caulfield's cook, Charlene, is probably Black but never actually appears in the novel.) "Colored" was not only an acceptable term to use when referring to an African-American, but it was preferred in the 1940's. "Negro" was the label of preference in the 1920's and continued to be used frequently until the early 1960's, but "colored" had gained favor within civil rights organizations by the end of the depression. *The National Association for the Advancement of Colored People* (1909) changed its name from *The*

National Negro Committee in 1910 in part because the term "colored" was deemed more inclusive.

Page 201: "...Fuck you..."

This is the only one of the many well-known "four-letter" obscenities to appear in *The Catcher in the Rye*. Readers in 1951 had only just begun to see this and other common expletives in print. James Joyce's *Ulysses* was banned from the country until 1933. Norman Mailer's *The Naked and the Dead* (1949) had been banned in Canada, and James Jones' *From Here to Eternity* stirred up its own share of controversy when it was published in the same year as *The Catcher in the Rye* . Aside from the six times *"Fuck you "* appears in chapter 25 - with the "F" always capitalized, by the way - readers in 1949 were more appalled by Holden's casual blasphemy exemplified by his frequent use of "goddam" and "Christ".

Page 201: "...to take a leak..."

To urinate; take a piss; take a leak; pee; see a man about a dog; spend a penny, whiz.

Page 202: "...recess yard...walked over to the museum..."

Phoebe's school is just across *Fifth Avenue* from the *Metropolitan Museum of Art*. Salinger's apparent model is the Dalton School, now located at 108 East 89th Street.

Originally located in Massachusetts and called the Children's University School, the first Dalton School open in 1919 on West 74th Street. Later, when more expansive facilities were required, the school relocated the Lower (elementary) campus to West 74nd Street and the Upper to its current location at 108 East 89th Street. Today, students in kindergarten through the third grade attend classes at "Little Dalton" on 91st Street between Park and Madison Avenues, fourth through twelfth grades meet at "Big Dalton" on East 89th Street. A separate facility on 87th Street and Third Avenue is used for physical education. All of these locations fall within the range of Holden's wanderings on the Monday morning prior to his hospitalization.

The Dalton Plan, devised by educational progressive Helen Parkhurst, was a forward-thinking humanistic approach to the education of young people. Parkhurst's model, developed in part through an association with educational innovator Maria Montessori, sought to design each student's program with an eye toward meeting his or her needs, enhancing his or her unique skills and promoting independence while fostering a sense of shared, community values. Though Parkhurst's Plan has been substantially altered over the years, the essential framework of the institution she sought to establish is still in evidence and many of the school traditions she established carried on to this day. The structural framework she devised, which remains intact, consists of three parts: House, Assignment and Lab.

The Dalton School, part of the Ivy Preparatory School league, has a worldwide reputation for excellence and educational innovation, though critics would attribute at least part of its success to its rigorous and highly selective acceptance procedure. In addition, The Dalton School is beyond the financial reach of all but the most privileged families.

Page 203 "...my brudda..."

My brother; a pronunciation common to parts of New York and New Jersey.

Page 204: "...yella streak a mile wide..."

Cowardly.

(See **Chapter 13 "...one of those very yellow guys."**)

Page 204: "...sort of had diarrhea...sort of passed out..."

More symptoms of a panic attack.

(See this chapter page 248 **"...don't let me disappear."** And **Chapter 20, page 219: "...started chattering like hell..."**)

Page 205: "...the only reason I'd leave my cabin and come back."

Holden's comment is more interesting to modern readers than it might have been in 1951. In the mid-1950's, wearied of public attention and intimidated by the success of *The Catcher in The Rye*, J.D. Salinger went into seclusion in Cornish, New Hampshire. While it is known that he continued writing, he no

Hello? Anyone home and not working with explosives?

longer published, granted interviews nor traveled outside his immediate environment. Though Harper Lee, author of *To Kill a Mockingbird* , did much the same thing, she was less reclusive and certainly more responsive to fans and well-wishers.

Salinger's "I'd prefer not to" response to notoriety is viewed as increasingly odd in an age when people who have accomplished absolutely nothing in their lives are daily thrust upon us by the media.

Page 205: "...she was just coming across Fifth Avenue..."

Holden sees Phoebe across Fifth Avenue at 82nd Street on her way from school.

(See this chapter, page 251: **"...recess yard...walked over to the museum..."**)

Page 206: "I got sort of dizzy"

Another symptom of a panic attack.

(See this chapter, page 252: **"...sort of had diarrhea...sort of passed out..."**; also **page 248 "...don't let me disappear."**; and **Chapter 20, page 219: "...started chattering like hell..."**)

Page 208: "take a walk down to the zoo?"

Central Park has had a small zoo since 1864. At the turn of the century the zoo housed more than 500 animals in conditions modern visitors would find appalling. Enclosures were dark, barren concrete and steel pens in which unfortunate specimens lived out short, squalid lives - actually, much like New York's immigrant population at the time. The zoo was extensively

Seal enclosure, Central Park Menagerie, 1950

renovated in the 1930's and again in the 1980's. There are still seals there, and bears too. The zoo is located on the east side of the park between 63rd and 65th Streets; eighteen blocks from the *Metropolitan Museum of Art*. From there it is a short walk up to the Dairy and through Playmates Arch to the carousel.

Page 210: "...crossed over this little street...through one of those tunnels...on the way ..."

The "little tunnel" is most likely *Playmates Arch*.

On the dust jacket of the first edition of this novel in 1851 (see page 7) was artist Michael Mitchell's two-color print of a carousel horse above smaller drawings of Central Park with skyscrapers in the background. The top half of the cover is dominated by a simple wood or linoleum block print, in brick red, over an ecru background. The details of the horse and the park scene are drawn in with pen and ink. The title, *The Catcher in the Rye*, appears in two lines of yellow block lettering across the top of the cover over the red portion. The back of the dust jacket originally carried a photograph of the author, but this was eliminated at the author's request on subsequent editions.

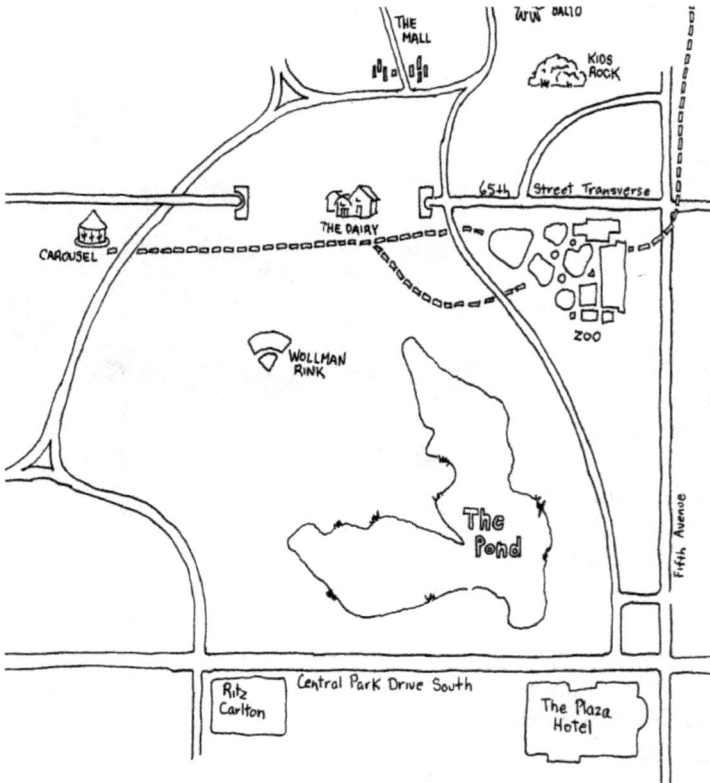

Map of the southeast corner of Central Park showing
Holden and Phoebe's route from the Museum of Natural
History down Fifth Avenue and two possible ways to exit
the zoo toward the carousel.

Page 210: "...the carrousel."

At it's most basic, a carousel is a revolving circular platform on
which are mounted representations of animals, usually horses,
which are ridden to the accompaniment of music. Sometimes
the carousel (Salinger prefers the variant spelling with two r's)
is known as a *merry-go-round* or *roundabout*. The name comes
directly from the French *carrousel* and the Italian *carosello*, a

Though the costumes predate Holden by about 70 years, the carousel he was familiar with looked a lot more like this one than the one that is in the park today.

tournament in which horsemen display equestrian skills in an arena.

The carousel Holden and Phoebe visit burned down in 1950, a year before the publication of *The Catcher in the Rye,* lending a poignant - and probably intentional - irony to the melody playing while Phoebe rides, *"Smoke Gets in Your Eyes".* It had replaced an earlier one that also burned. There is still a nice carrousel in Central Park, but it is an imported replacement built in 1908 as a Coney Island attraction and moved to the

Central Park site in 1952. The Friedsam Memorial Carousel is adjacent to Playmates Arch and the 65th Street Transverse in the southwest quadrant of the Park.

American carousels revolved to the accompaniment of music provided by elaborate band-organs manufactured by Armitage-Herschell, Armitage Factories, Stinson, Wurlitzer and Germany-based Ruth & Sohn. The last two names are the most familiar to carousel fans in the United States. The old Wurlitzer and Ruth & Sohn mechanical bands are marvelous instruments - actually collections of instruments - and there is no music in the world quite as wonderfully magical as theirs. At its heart each pneumatic band organ had a precision-tuned set of up to 350 pipes. As versatile as any ballpark or cathedral organ, these instruments could howl like a train, whistle like a piccalo, groan like bagpipes, fart like a bull or toot like a tug. Augmenting this air orchestra was a set of bells, a small marimba-like arrangement of graduated tone-bars, and a full size bass drum. The color and dynamic range of this ensemble was immense. The unexpected grace notes ringing at the treble end and gut-startling thumps at the other made for dazzlingly impressive renditions of popular and classical melodies. Though many carefully maintained carousels around the world still have the original band organs intact the equipment is very old and in need of regular maintenance by skilled craftspeople. Sadly, in many instances carousels display them as unplayable antiques or use them only on special occasions substituting wholly unacceptable recorded music. A real shame.

Page 210: "Oh, Marie!"

An Italian song made popular in America during the 1940's. The original lyric, at least in part, goes like this:

> Devo guardare fuori dalla finestra.
> Fammi affacciare, Maria
> che stai in mezzo alla strada
> ed é tutto da vedere...

I'm sure the Italian is charming, but rather than go with a straight translation the English lyricist kept it short and in the vernacular:

Oh Marie, oh Marie,
In your arms, I am longing to be
Oh Baby, tell me you love me
Just kiss me once
While the stars shine above me
Hey Marie, oh Marie
In your arms, I am longing to be
Oh Baby, tell me you love me
Hey Marie.

Page 211: "Smoke Gets in Your Eyes"

In spite of some awkwardness in the lyrics, the song *"Smoke Gets in Your Eyes"* has proven to be very popular since its debut in the Jerome Kern and Otto Harbach musical, *Roberta*, in 1933. The Broadway stage production was a mild success with a fine cast including Fred MacMurray, Bob Hope, George Murphy, Fay Templeton and Sydney Greenstreet. A 1935 film version starred Irene Dunne, Fred Astaire, Ginger Rogers and Randolph Scott. Most audiences came to *Roberta* for the songs including "I Won't Dance" and "Lovely to Look At".

Originally sung on stage by Tamara (Tamara Drasin, 1910-1943) *"Smoke Gets in Your Eyes"* has been interpreted by scores of singers since including *Ruth Etting* who reached #17 on the Billboard chart in 1934; *The Platters*, who had a #1 hit with it in 1959 and *Blue Haze, #27 in 1973.*

The Otto Harbach lyric goes like this:

> *They asked me how I knew*
> *My true love was true*
> *I of course replied*
> *Something here inside*
> *Cannot be denied.*
> *They said someday you'll find*
> *All who love are blind*
> *When your heart's on fire,*
> *You must realize*
> *Smoke gets in your eyes.*
> *So I chaffed them*
> *And I gaily laughed to think*
> *They could doubt my love.*
> *Yet today my love has flown away,*
> *I am without my love.*
> *Now laughing friends deride*
> *Tears I cannot hide*
> *So I smile and say*
> *When a lovely flame dies,*
> *Smoke gets in your eyes.*

"Smoke Gets in Your Eyes" and *"Oh, Marie"* are unusual musical pieces for a carousel; marches, waltzes, rags and folk tunes were always popular. The band organs that accompanied these old carousels played from Wurlitzer music rolls or folded cardboard sheets and only occasionally included contemporary tunes.

Page 211: "...gold ring..."

In the early days of mechanical carousels European and American riders could try, if they wished, to grab a brass or

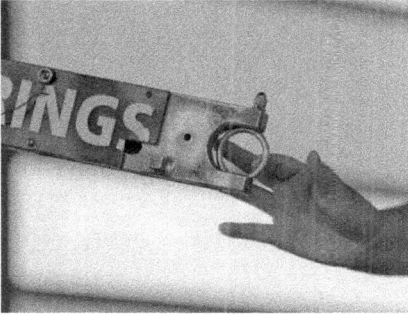

gold-painted metal ring which was suspended just out of reach to one side of the revolving menagerie. Successfully snatching the ring meant a free ride or a small prize. Failure often meant the embarrassment of falling headlong into a pile of straw or wood chips before scores of laughing on-lookers. Obviously, short-armed riders were at a disadvantage. It has been speculated that abuse of the system by escaped chimpanzees and orangutans led to the eventual discontinuation of this game, but more likely it was a casualty of costly liability insurance .

Up until the end of the twentieth century the phrase "catch (or grab) the brass ring" was still commonly used to signify a risk that has paid off handsomely.

Chapter 26

(Several weeks after the events described in Chapter 25)

In which Holden ends his tale.

> "Pure life's courage drink!" cried he:
> "This advice to prize then learn,--
> Never to this place return
> > Johann Wolfgang Von Goethe, 1797
> > (trans. E.A. Bowring)

Page 213: "...how I got sick and all..."

It is never made clear whether Holden understands the nature or causes of his breakdown. He uses no clinical or therapeutic language in his retelling of the events that preceded his hospitalization. And, though he has obviously spent some time in a therapeutic environment it is clear from the story he has st told that there are aspects of his pre-hospitalization experiences with which he still has not come to

Illustration from John Bunyan's **The Pilgrim's Progress, 1678**

grips or achieved any real understanding of. He appears only slightly less emotionally fragile than he had been the winter before the "madman stuff" began, yet he expects to be discharged soon. Is Holden ready to go back to school? Is he ready to return to his home, parents or sister? This uncertainty leaves the reader with at least a soupcon of guarded optimism.

Index

Photographic and Art Credits

All photographs and photographically reproduced images used in this book are freely available in the Public Domain, licensed under Creative Commons Attribution 2.0, or available through GNU Free Documentation License with the following exception(s):

Reproductions of film posters, Video or DVD cover art is made possible through United States Fair use laws

Though these images may be subject to copyright, their use is covered by the U.S. fair use laws because:

They do not limit limit the copyright owner's rights to sell the films in any way, in fact, use may encourage sales.

They are low resolution copies of a Film Poster / VHS or DVD Cover.

They do not limit limit the copyright owner's rights to sell the films in any way, in fact, use may encourage sales.

Because of the low resolution, copies could not be used to make illegal copies of the artwork/image.

The image is itself a subject of discussion in the book or used to significantly augment the purpose or function of the book.

The images are significant because they were used to promote notable films.

With grateful appreciation to the Wikipedia Commons photographic archive.

Original pen and ink illustrations by Phiz Cruikshank Hogarth Dore II
Copyright © 2009 Phiz Dore Inc.

www.ingramcontent.com/pod-product-compliance
Lightning Source LLC
Chambersburg PA
CBHW060010050426
42448CB00012B/2685